ARSENE WENGER
FIFTY DEFINING FIXTURES

Layth Yousif

AMBERLEY

To my three Junior Gunners –
Charlotte, William and Josie.
And to Claire, my rock.

First published 2014

Amberley Publishing
The Hill, Stroud
Gloucestershire, GL5 4EP

www.amberley-books.com

Copyright © Layth Yousif, 2014

British Library Cataloguing in Publication Data.
A catalogue record for this book is available from the British Library.

ISBN 978 1 4456 4221 5 (print)
ISBN 978 1 4456 4243 7 (ebook)

Typesetting and Origination by Amberley Publishing.
Printed in the UK.

Contents

Foreword

What attracted me to make my seismic move across North London from N17 to N5 was the thought of playing with truly great players in a truly great team, the challenge to win top trophies year in, year out, while competing in a gloriously attacking side that also contained as many warriors as it did winners.

In short, a team led by Arsène Wenger.

I was fortunate enough to win many medals while playing for Arsène, and it is my sincere belief that one day people will look back at the Arsenal side of 2003/04 – the Invincibles team – and say, 'Do you know what? That was a once in lifetime team.'

There were many leaders in that side, tough players who played for the badge, the club, the team, and most importantly, for each other. Equally, we had numerous skilful, attacking players that struck fear into many an opposition's defence. And we should never forget it was a team that was assembled by Arsène Wenger, who along with Herbert Chapman is arguably the most important manager in Arsenal's proud history, and certainly one of the most successful.

Quite simply, I am proud to have played for Arsenal, proud to have played with many of the players I did, and proud to have played under Arsène Wenger, and this book brings back a lot of memories of my time in the red and white.

I have got to know Layth as a journalist who has interviewed me for the *London Evening Standard*, *The Gooner* and *Sabotage Times*, and what has struck me is his love, knowledge and passion for Arsenal Football Club. I hope this shines through in this excellent book that has brought back a lot special of memories for me of playing under Arsène Wenger for the club. I hope it also brings back many special memories for you too. This book is a must-read for Arsenal fans everywhere.

Sol Campbell
July 2014

Introduction

All it actually took for Arsenal to cement their place as one of the biggest clubs in world football was for one man to revolutionise our beloved institution. That man was Arsène Wenger.

When he arrived, we didn't even own our own training ground, the players often having to play second fiddle to university football teams at London Colney. When the team played on a rare trip to the United States, Gunners stalwart Ken Frair was asked by a brash American: 'We've got 25,000 parking spaces around our stadium – how many you guys got?' Only for modest Ken to answer: 'Sixty.' The man was hushed into silence. '60,000? Now that it amazing.' Mr Friar shuffled his feet before answering honestly, if a tad sheepishly, 'No, sixty.'

Now we have a state-of-the-art stadium, which is sold out for every game, with our only debts being manageable ones owing to the stadium. We have won eight trophies under Wenger, including three titles, two doubles and five FA Cups, not forgetting we were the first London team to appear in the Champions League final, with our heroic ten-man team only 17 minutes from eternal glory against the best team in the world.

We have qualified for the Champions League a record seventeen years in succession, and we are respected throughout the planet for our superb attacking football, hailed for our attacking players, for our genuine commitment to playing football, and for our insistence on raising young players to play the right way – the number of Arsenal youngsters Wenger has nurtured, who despite not making the grade at our club, have gone on to make a career in professional, is astounding.

He also created a team that emulated a feat not achieved in English football for 116 years, and has sculpted teams and players that will live on forever in the memory.

All these laudable ideals occurred because our board, in late summer 1996, had the far-sightedness to appoint a bespectacled Frenchman who had no prior experience of English football either as a player or a manager, and who was plying his trade in far off Japan at the time. On paper, the decision to appoint Arsène Wenger seemed incredulous, bordering on madness – but, my word, what an era it heralded.

For someone like myself, a season ticket holder for thirty years, and one who has attended the majority of Wenger's 1,000-plus fixtures, to whittle down the number to a mere fifty was extremely hard. The number of conversations I have had with fellow Gooner friends on the subject has provoked fierce debate.

Every game means something special to somebody – but what I have tried to do is write about the ones that had a far greater impact on the club. Fixtures that symbolised an era, a time, an ethos; fixtures that explained a strategy; fixtures that a won trophy; fixtures that lost a trophy; fixtures that told the story of a season; fixtures that were a snapshot of a rivalry; fixtures that would never be forgotten – for good or bad. In short, Arsène Wenger's fifty defining fixtures.

You may not agree with my all my choices – in truth I wouldn't expect you to – but what I would hope this book and my writing will do is to prompt some discussions of your own, and help recall some good memories. So read on to find out which matches made my list – and why.

And if you'd like to discuss it further please follow me @laythy29 and tweet me using the hashtag #AW50, and let me know which games you think I should have included.

In the meantime, I hope you enjoy the memories this book prompted, as much as I did when writing it.

Layth Yousif
July 2014

Sheffield Wednesday (H)

17 September 1996

The 1996 Arsenal AGM was held in the first week of September in one of Highbury's distinguished oak-panelled rooms. Normally a placid affair interspersed with the rubber stamping of minor points of order, the meeting held that year was one of the fieriest and most tempestuous anybody could remember.

Shareholders, the majority of them long-standing supporters of the club, were up in arms over the way the previous managerial incumbent, Bruce Rioch, had been relieved of his duties. They were also concerned at the lack of visible movement from the club on appointing a new manager.

The chairman, Old Etonian Peter Hill-Wood, the latest of three generations of his family to run the club, and a City man to the core, was unused to such open hostility. He told the many disaffected stakeholders, in words that would come to be seen as prophetic and visionary, yet seemed anything but on that day, 'We have acted in the best interests of the club. We have identified a replacement of considerable reputation who has agreed to join us. We cannot announce his appointment officially, as we have given an undertaking not to do so.'

In a touch of farce, which eventually brought comic relief to the fraught proceedings a voice from the floor asked innocently, 'An undertaking to who, Mr Chairman?'

Without thinking, the dignified custodian of Arsenal, whose family connections to Arsenal stretched back to the early years of the twentieth century, and whose usual idea of a crisis was when the half-time port ran dry, immediately replied, 'An undertaking to Mr Wenger of course.'

Cue much laughter, which almost drowned out what he said next, 'We expect him to be with us by the end of September,' adding, ominously for the club's rivals but which was virtually ignored at the time, 'We have acquired two new players, Patrick Vieira and Rémi Garde. Our ambitions are to get the right squad and win another trophy or two.'

Mr Hill-Woods' words may have been offered as a placatory submission, but as the years went on, they appeared more like a clarion call in the first steps of reviving a great club that had lost its way somewhat, turning it into a global super power.

Arsène Wenger's arrival at Arsenal, the worst-kept secret in football, was confirmed on Monday 17 September. The same evening the rudderless club were due to take on Sheffield Wednesday.

Strictly speaking, Monsieur Wenger's tenure was not to begin until 30 September.

But the symbolic contrast between the opening 28 minutes of this game, and the remainder, imbued as it was by the spirit of Wenger's first signing, was hugely emblematic of the sea change to occur at this grand old London institution, for so long derided as an unadventurous, conformist and cautious establishment.

In the words of the Irish poet YB Yeats: 'All changed, changed utterly.'

Arsenal: Seaman, Bould, Linighan, Keown, Dixon, Parlour, Merson, Platt, Winterburn, Wright, Hartson. Substitute: Vieira for Parlour.
Sheffield Wednesday: Pressman, Atherton, Walker, Stefanovic, Nolan, Collins, Whittingham, Pembridge, Blinker, Hirst, Booth. Substitutes: Nicol for Stefanovic, Trustfull for Whittingham, Oakes for Blinker.
Referee: Mike Reed
Attendance: 33,461

On the morning of the game, Martin Thorpe wrote in *The Guardian*: 'Football's worst kept secret was finally confirmed yesterday when it was formally announced that Arsène Wenger is Arsenal's new manager.'

Wenger, speaking at a press conference in Japan, said, 'It is my dream to manage a team in a top level European league. And if I don't accept the offer right now I will miss the chance.'

In words that seem almost trite at the time but are now viewed as visionary and prescient, he added, 'I think Arsenal is a club with big potential. I think that English football is going up and that the Premiership is one of the most important leagues in the world now.

'So I think that it also was a challenge for me to be maybe the first foreign manager – and for sure the first Frenchman – to go there and be successful.'

In 1996, Wenger was coming to a country where John Major was still Prime Minister, the national consciousness was still coming to terms with the terrible massacre at Dunblane, and the devastating Manchester bombing. Genetically modified food had been introduced and the Spice Girls had just been dethroned after seven weeks at number one with 'Wanabee'.

In the match against Sheffield Wednesday at Highbury on 17 September 1996, Wenger's first signing made an immediate impact, giving the newly confirmed manager vitally important breathing space and goodwill.

Gunners stalwart and legend Pat Rice who, as Wenger's loyal and trusted right-hand man would add another seventeen years to make an incredible total of forty-four years spent at Arsenal Football Club, had taken temporary charge of the team ahead of the Frenchman's arrival. The previous provisional incumbent Stewart Houston had realised his time was up and resigned the previous Friday, to take over from Ray Wilkins at Queens Park Rangers.

Michael Hart writing in the *London Evening Standard* noted, 'When Arsène Wenger appeared on the big video screens at Highbury, addressing the fans before kick-off, you sensed a new chapter was about to begin.'

There was an element of French farce about proceedings prior to kick-off as the match was delayed for 25 minutes due to a power failure. The turmoil seemed appropriate for a club that needed strong direction on and off the pitch. The club once boasted four manages in forty-seven years. Now, with Wenger set to assume charge, it was four in seven weeks – albeit two temporary ones.

Wednesday began the livelier. Andy Booth netted after 25 minutes, with David Hirst striking the bar shortly afterwards. But it was an injury to Ray Parlour, a man who would be transformed by Wenger's arrival. In an interview with the author for the *Gooner* fanzine Parlour humbly admitted, 'I owe Wenger so much for transforming my career', which formulated the first official footballing stimulus from Arsène Wenger to Arsenal FC.

As Michael Hart noted for *The Standard*:

Arsenal had looked sadly inept in the first half ... but after the interval Patrick Vieira began to take charge and expose Wednesday's defensive flaws. The big Frenchman, making his debut as a substitute for Ray Parlour looks a quality player though he still has to adjust to the pace of the English game.

David Lacey concurred in his *Guardian* match report afterwards:

It is safe to say that Arsène Wenger will find managing Arsenal a novel experience. Certainly last night they showed just how hard they are to put down. For much of the first half they were out-thought, outpaced and outmanoeuvred. They fell behind to Andy Booth's goal after 25 minutes and could have been three down by the half hour ... but Rice introduced a portentous Gallic influence, Vieira, Arsenal's £3.5 million signing from Milan.

With his deceptively powerful, long telescoped legs, perfectly designed to complement an athletic technique sometimes overlooked, and matched with a tremendous will to win, Patrick Vieira was the ideal signing for a moribund Arsenal team. And the perfect introduction on such a night. His immediate influence played a huge role in persuading fans and critics alike that the Arsenal board had made the right decision. For if the young Frenchman had not had such a bright start, if he had performed dismally for example, many would have been questioning Wenger from the start. As it was, his appearance was the original defining moment, in a defining match for Wenger.

Fans watched with an all too obvious delight as Wenger's man Vieira bossed the midfield, breaking up play effectively by winning the ball from the opposition and using it intelligently, either by driving forward or feeding a better-placed teammate. His power, laced with finesse, was a revelation that night to the club's long-suffering supporters.

On 61 minutes, Des Walker fouled Paul Merson in the box. Merson, who was also having a good night, gave the ball to Ian Wright, who easily slotted home past Kevin Pressman.

Twelve minutes into the second half, David Platt made a typical lung bursting run into the box to meet John Hartson's low cross to put the re-energised Gunners 2-1 up.

Wright then tapped in from Platt's pass for his second to make it 3-1, before netting his hat-trick shortly afterwards to make it 4-1.

Replicating the *Evening Standard* bill poster around the day of Wenger's arrival asking the question many were no doubt thinking, albeit a shade too bluntly: 'Arsène Who?', Wright was asked post-match what he thought of Wenger.

Whether Arsenal's dynamic forward, whose hat-trick on the night took him to 100 league goals for the club and his 150th in only 226 games, had his tongue firmly in his cheek, he playfully replied, 'Who?' Yet after the introduction of Wenger's man Vieira, which changed the game, everyone now knew who Wenger was.

As Pat Rice said when appraising Wenger's match-altering signing, 'the fans got a chance tonight to see what Patrick can do and I think the fans loved him,' adding with an astute far-sightedness and deadly conviction, 'Patrick will be a big star here one day. I've also no doubt Arsène will prove himself in English football.'

How right he was on both counts.

Blackburn Rovers (A)

12 October 1996

It is a common misconception that the *London Evening Standard* wrote in the newspaper, 'Arsène Who?' on the day of Wenger's arrival. Being a freelancer at the esteemed paper, I know that the erroneous belief is still a bone of contention in certain circles. What actually occurred was that the headline appeared as a bill poster, which is somewhat different.

Yet, as the days until Wenger's first official match in charge ticked down, there was still a considerable lack of awareness about the Frenchman entering English football for the first time. A feature article in the *Standard* dated 18 September 1996 asked the question:

How should the name be pronounced —both of them? If you are French, you will probably address him as *Ar-senn Won-jair*. German? *Ar-sehn Ven-ger*, perhaps. North Bank regular, plasterer Trevor Hale, struggled slightly: *'Arse-in Won-gah, innit mate?'*

Football men were queuing up to have their say. The respected Trevor Brooking told the *Standard*:

Arsène Wenger will require all his expertise if he is to salvage something form Arsenal's season. The Frenchman will take over a club in disarray and he must quickly impose his personality on all aspects of the club so that no one is in any doubt who is in actual charge.

Don Howe, the ex-Arsenal player, manager and coach said perceptively, 'Sooner or later a continental manager is going to break through and have success in England'.

Prior to the Blackburn game, Wenger said,

I am not here because of friendship with the board but because the board considered I have the best qualities to do the job. I'm very conscious of the need to win over the fans. I don't think they'll reject me just because I'm a foreign coach, but they will reject me if I don't do a good job.

I want to keep the great strengths of Arsenal – the spirit of the players. For this we have to keep the majority of the players English – and not just buy big stars. I want to give the players here a chance.

I like to win and I try every day to be better than the day before.

For Arsenal fans worried about the direction of their club it was music to their ears, especially after the team had been knocked out in Cologne against Borussia Mönchengladbach in the first round of the UEFA Cup.

Michael Hart of *The Standard* wrote,

> Wenger knows whatever his long term ambitions, the priority must be to restore the sort of defensive stability that made Arsenal one of Europe's most successful teams ... what is worrying in losing to Borussia Mönchengladbach is that at their best under George Graham and his assistant Stewart Houston, Arsenal met a lot of accomplished teams in Europe – Paris Saint-Germain, Parma, Auxerre and Sampdoria. They were probably technically superior but Arsenal were able to beat them all because of the defensive discipline. That was not the case against Borussia and Wenger will need to address that problem if Arsenal are to get back into the big time.

It was a defeat I witnessed. Wenger issued tactical instructions at half-time with the team winning 2-1, directing Pat Rice to change the formation from 3-5-2 to an English 4-4-2. The attendant 3-2 loss in the second half meant that Wenger needed to hit the ground running in his first official game in Lancashire. The history of English football and Arsenal FC could have been so different if he hadn't. As Wenger said with huge resonance on the eve of the game: 'Names come and go. But people remember those who bring results. Judge me by my work.'

Blackburn: Flowers, Kenna, Sherwood, Bohinen, Wilcox, Marker, Sutton, Berg, Donis, Beattie, Croft. Substitutes: Ripley for Donis, Gudmundsson for Wilcox. Not used: Given, Flitcroft, Broomess.
Arsenal: Seaman, Dixon, Keown, Bould, Adams, Winterburn, Platt, Vieira, Merson, Wright, Hartson. Substitutes: Parlour for Hartson. Not used: Shaw, Linighan, Rose, Lukic
Referee: Steve Dunn.
Attendance: 24,303

Reflecting the feeling of many at the time, Hart also wrote, 'Arsenal will not thank me for saying this but, based on the achievements of the handful of foreign coaches to have worked in England, they are taking something of a gamble with Wenger,' before adding with insight, 'but if he is successful, the foreign coaches will soon be following the foreign players to these shores.'

It is hard to understand just how much of a revolutionary act Arsenal took in appointing Wenger. Yet the process that had begun tentatively against Sheffield Wednesday the previous month, and which would officially commence with the away game at Ewood Park, would eventually lead to such a transformation of Arsenal and English football in general that English football should almost be labelled 'BW' and 'AW' – before Wenger and after Wenger.

Quite simply, he modernised English football; first raising the domestic game at the top level into parity with far more open-minded and technically advanced continental leagues, then with the help of Sky Television money, far surpassed them, certainly in the first half of his tenure. This came through improved diets, through scientific training programmes designed to maximise potential, through a greater understanding of athletes' bodies, through commitment to technical excellence and – perhaps the most important of all – an undying belief in the way the beautiful game should be played.

Specific to Arsenal FC, with a nod to the tireless innovation shown by one of his Highbury antecedents – Herbert Chapman – Wenger designed and built the club's state-of-the-art training ground, and played a huge part in moving the club literally across the road to a cutting edge 60,000-capacity super-stadium. In doing so, Wenger made the club one of the biggest in the world, with match-day revenues that far exceeded their London rivals – bolstered as they were to be by injections of oligarch or tax exiles money – so much so that the club's incomes were only dwarfed by three of the world's biggest clubs, Manchester United, Real Madrid and their Catalan rivals Barcelona.

Wenger recalled years later how much of a culture shock that first day had been in terms of the players' diets and food intake. He said, 'At the first match, the players were chanting "we want our Mars bars!" At half-time I asked my physio, Gary Lewin, "Nobody is talking, what's wrong with them?" and he replied, "They're hungry". I hadn't given them their chocolate before the game!'

And to think, the road to all this started at humble Ewood Park on a dull October's Saturday in 1996.

The Wenger revolution began in style after just 180 seconds through a player who, while initially wary of the new boss, came to love him as much as anyone as he fully bought into the Frenchman's pioneering ethos.

Ian Wright's goal, the first of thousands for a Wenger-led Arsenal team, exposed if not 4,000 holes in Rovers' defence in Blackburn, then at least one fatal gap in their hopes.

The move involved another stalwart, who would go on to have his career extended by Le Professor's method, as he was known in the early years – Nigel Winterburn crossed to big John Hartson, who nodded the ball back across Blackburn's 6 yard box. Wright, who had been snubbed for the forthcoming England *v.* Poland World Cup qualifying game at Wembley, had a point to prove to all and sundry. He made it by selecting his spot before striking the ball cleanly past Tim Flowers, who could do nothing to prevent it.

It was 1-0 to Arsenal. It was a refrain from the George Graham years. But the match proved no journalists would ever again call for a return of those years, fearful of what Wenger would bring to an unsettled club.

The second goal was even better. Six minutes after the interval, Vieira, whose performance against Sheffield Wednesday crucially allayed a considerable amount of doubt about Wenger among the fans, sent a superb diagonal cross-field pass to Wright. Thirty-three-year-old Wright, as motivated as he had ever been, burst past Gary Croft, and as Flowers came out to narrow the angle, dismissively smashed it over him from inches inside the box.

The Sun's headline was: 'Wenger a Wright winner – Ian's two hot says Wenger.' They went on to say breathlessly, 'The Frenchman has walked into Highbury as the fourth boss in two years amid a backdrop of bungs, bust ups and managers being ruthlessly shown the door.' But Wenger insisted, 'I've been at other big clubs where football was just work, but at Arsenal I have seen real friendship among the players'.

Afterwards, Wenger confirmed his commitment to his players, a philosophy he continues daily to his men, saying of Wright's excellent performance:

They were great goals. He has the quality finish you very rarely see. Wright has the touch and he produces it at the right moment. It is why he is Ian Wright. He is a world-class striker. I am only finding out about life here but it is a pity he started his career later than he should have.

The performance and result boded well for Wenger.

Not content with praising Wright, he also lauded his new team saying, 'It was about discipline, solidarity and organisation,' before going on to charm the rest of the country by adding, 'I like the British, I like the feeling in the stadiums. It was a good day.'

For Arsène Wenger, his team and their anxious fans, it certainly was.

Tottenham Hotspur (H)

24 November 1996

Arsène Wenger recalled his first few months in charge:

> At that time, what Arsenal did, you needed to be a little bit crazy. Crazy in the sense that I had no name, I was foreign, there was no history. They needed to be, maybe not crazy, but brave.
>
> I can show some articles where people tried to prove that the foreign managers can never win an English championship. That has changed. There was a history and belief in England that the foreign manager could not be successful. Now you have a different feeling, now you think only foreign managers can be successful. That is wrong as well.
>
> People were asking who I was. I was a complete unknown. And there was no history of a foreign manager succeeding in England. So I was in a situation where no one knew me and history was against me.

The day history started to turn in Wenger's favour was arguably his first North London derby less than two months after taking charge.

A goalless draw at home to Coventry City the week after his bow at Ewood Park was notable only for an incident between Ian Wright and Coventry goalkeeper Steve Ogrizovic, resulting in the Sky Blues' 'keeper receiving a broken nose. Wenger's first month concluded with a 3-0 win over Leeds United at Highbury. It was symbolic as the defeat was inflicted on former manager George Graham, who was making his managerial return to Highbury.

Wenger's team ended October joint top of the table with Newcastle United, both on twenty-four points in eleven games.

Arsenal's first fixture of November was against the Crazy Gang of Wimbledon at Selhurst Park, which saw an eagerly contested game end 2-2 (Wright, Merson). An unfortunate Nigel Winterburn own goal against Manchester United at Old Trafford curtailed Alex Ferguson's run of three matches without a win. It also promulgated the Gunners, miserable streak of failing to score at Old Trafford since the Premier League commenced.

Wenger said afterwards, 'Obviously, the way we lost was difficult to accept, but I'm happy with the way we played. Our organisation was excellent, we kept fighting and I am very optimistic for the future.'

The immediate future was his first North London derby. As he told the assembled press the day before, who were beginning to enjoy the way he elegantly and expansively expounded his views on football matters:

For me, being creative is scoring goals. Beauty is efficiency. It is not about making nice movements. The crowd love Patrick Vieira because he does the right thing at the right moment, not because he's beautiful to watch. I see players who do wonderful things outside a match but once in a match they are disasters because they cannot do them when they are needed.

Wenger also touched upon the delicate matter of captain Tony Adams' alcoholism. Wenger grew up in his parents' bar in Alsace, developing a lifelong distain for alcohol yet was sensitive enough to recognise the addiction it causes in people:

The real revelation of a player's character is not in his social life but in how he plays. In my social life I can hide my real personality, but when I am playing I show how I really am. For me being a professional is not just playing once a week, and playing well from time to time – it's trying to be your best every time. For this you need a strong mentality. For professionals it is not normal every day to get up and say, 'OK, let's get on with the fight.' You need a special attitude. Winners are those able to do it. When you have players like I have who have been doing it for ten years, that means there is something special inside them which makes them want to win.

His warriors showed him their winning desire on a filthy North London November afternoon – and how.

Arsenal: Lukic, Dixon, Keown, Bould, Adams, Winterburn, Platt, Vieira, Merson, Wright, Bergkamp. Substitutes: Hartson for Platt (80), Parlour for Bergkamp (90). Not used: Linighan, Morrow, Bartram.
Spurs: Walker, Howells, Calderwood, Nielsen, Anderton, Sheringham, Armstrong, Wilson, Campbell, Carr, Sinton. Substitutes: Baardsen, Edinburgh, Fox, Nethercott, Allen.
Referee: David Elleray
Attendance: 38,264

The next morning's *Daily Mirror* report, by the man whose reporting of Tony Adams scoring at both ends at Old Trafford in an important 1-1 draw on the way to the 1988/89 League title saw someone put donkey ears onto the Arsenal legend, went some way to making amends for that ignorant and unnecessary slur:

Tony Adams scored one of the best goals of his career with the touch of a Baresi or a Beckenbauer. For the new-look Adams, it was a sweet moment that turned this North London derby. He struck a beautiful left-foot volley ... lionheart Adams gave a display that was worth ten out of ten in anybody's marking.
    Ian Wright waved his shirt above his head screaming with delight. But if there is one man who will savour the victory more than Adams it will be his manager Arsène Wenger.

It was a magnificent way to end a hotly contested North London derby played out in the driving rain, testing character as much as technique. The game had looked to be heading for a draw until Adams' intervention allowed his team to end the match as extremely worthy winners.

The Lilywhites may have argued they had the better of the opening 25 minutes, but Arsenal soon found their stride. The lively Merson fed Bergkamp, who fell after a clumsy challenge from Clive Wilson. The Dutchman, showing his reflexes, was up fastest, prompting a slow-witted Wilson to instinctively trip him with an extended leg. Wright then nailed the penalty far to the 'keeper's left before revealing a T-shirt that read 'I love the Lads'. It could be argued his tribute included his manager too.

The second period was only two minutes old when the Gunners could have been 2-0 up. Merson, involved again, lobbed a pass forward for Wright to run onto with only Walker to beat. To the disappointment of the Arsenal fans inside a raucous Highbury, he snatched at the shot with his left foot, dispatching the ball high over the bar.

Sheringham then kicked Lukic spitefully in the back as he lay on the ground. His cowardly actions prompted Arsenal's guardians of Keown, Dixon and Vieira to forcibly inform him not to do it again. Armstrong did nothing to abate the rising temperature by catching Vieira with a vicious two-footed lunge, from which the Frenchman was lucky to escape intact, and the Spurs man was fortunate to stay on the pitch. Lukic then saved form the resulting play before he threw the ball out of play to allow Vieira, who was still prone on the sodden pitch, to receive treatment.

However, Tottenham broke all respected convention as Neilsen from the throw in hurled the ball into Arsenal's box. The ball fell to Sinton, who fired the ball off the post and into the net off Lukic's shoulder.

Arsenal were understandably furious. Yet as the game seemed to be heading for a draw Spurs scarcely deserved, Bergkamp punished Spurs for the blatant cheating with a half-volleyed flick for Adams to joyfully slam into the net to the unabashed delight of the wet but hysterical Highbury crowd who idolised their leader.

With barely seconds remaining, and with the fans still celebrating the second goal, Wright looked to be allowing the clock to run down as he protected the ball near the visitor's right-hand corner. However, he then produced a moment of magic by befuddling the unfortunate Wilson, leaving him on the sodden turf before crossing for Bergkamp. The Dutchman then showed his deadly technique by moving the ball effortlessly from his left to his more powerful right foot, beating Carr in the process, before firing the ball across a despairing Walker and into the net. The crowd and his teammates went wild for the second time in minutes to prove there really was only one team in London.

Both late strikes were classics, sealing a classic result in Wenger's first North London derby that sent soaked Gooners home deliriously happy.

Afterwards Wenger said,

I am blessed with strong leaders. A good team without them would go nowhere but my aim is to keep Arsenal challenging for trophies.

My team constantly surprise me because they are better technically than I ever believed and we made a very strong finish.

Winning against Tottenham is the best moment of my time at Highbury so far.

Not many in the red-and-white half of North London would have disagreed with Wenger's happy assertion.

Leicester City (A)

27 August 1997

Arsenal's League campaign started on 9 August 1997, with a hard-fought 1-1 draw at Elland Road. Ian Wright netted his first goal of the season, before a defensive mix-up saw Jimmy Floyd Hasselbaink equalising for the home team. Two days later, at home to Coventry City, Wright scored both goals in Arsenal's 2-0 win. His brace left him a single goal from equalling Cliff Bastin's club goalscoring record of 178 goals, lasting since the 1930s.

Two goals – stunning strikes from Dennis Bergkamp and a debut goal by midfielder Marc Overmars – a week later saw the Gunners triumph on the South Coast 3-1 at Southampton.

The next match was at Filbert Street against Martin O'Neil's Leicester City. The Foxes had already won at Anfield and drawn at Old Trafford, but what was to follow was simply incredible.

Arsenal: Seaman, Dixon, Bould, Grimandi, Winterburn, Petit, Vieira, Parlour, Overmars, Bergkamp, Wright. Substitutes: Anelka for Wright (78), Platt for Parlour (82), Hughes for Overmars (82). Not used: Marshall, Lukic.
Leicester: Keller, Kaamark, Guppy, Elliott, Prior, Walsh, Izzet, Lennon, Savage, Claridge, Heskey. Substitutes: Fenton for Claridge, Cottee for Izzet, Parker for Savage (73). Not used: Andrews, Whitlow.
Referee: Graham Barber
Attendance: 21,089

The *Daily Mirror* match report the next morning read,

> Dutch master Dennis Bergkamp stunned Leicester City with a hat-trick, making it five goals in five days. But Leicester fought back to equalise in dramatic fashion. City 'keeper Kasey Keller had a sleepless night on the eve of the game as his wife gave birth to twins. But Bergkamp made sure he had another restless night by giving birth to three more goals to add to the two he scored at the Dell.

Dennis Bergkamp was unstoppable in this midweek away fixture in the East Midlands. The Dutchman opened the scoring in under 10 minutes with a perfectly executed curling strike into the top corner. The ex-Inter Milan player then doubled his tally with a second soon after the interval as Arsène Wenger's men appeared to be coasting to victory.

The North Londoners should have added to their lead as Bergkamp set up a half chance for Ian Wright with a high cross from the right to the back stick, where Wright attempted to volley home from 15 yards. Unfortunately, he sliced his effort wide much to the derision of the home fans inside a cramped but atmospheric Filbert Street.

Bergkamp then flicked the ball to striking partner Wright on the edge of the area. Wright spun a defender to fire a left -footed shot that flew narrowly wide.

It was Ray Parlour's turn to try and score with his rasping drive being pushed past the post by a desperate Keller, before Overmars fired a shot straight at the American moments later after coming inside.

But on 84 minutes, the Foxes commenced their fight back. Emile Heskey scored after David Platt missed his header. And in a hectic period of play moments after 90 minutes was showing on the clock, big centre-half Matt Elliott made it 2-2 in stoppage time.

However, Bergkamp, was far from finished. Fewer than sixty seconds after Elliott's leveller, David Platt, making amends for his error six minutes previously, saw Bergkamp running into the left-hand side of the box. The ex-Crewe and Inter Milan man then lifted an inch-perfect 40-yard pass into the Dutchman's path.

What happened next was as amazing as it was unbelievable. Bergkamp, who honed his technique as a child by kicking a ball against a set of railings for hours on end on a daily basis just so he could experience the ball coming to him from different angles, pulled the ball down with a gossamer-like touch. In the very same movement, he then flicked it with his left foot past Elliot. As the Foxes' defender fought his confusion at what was happening, he keenly jostled to recover his positioning in a futile attempt to block the ball, or Bergkamp. As he was doing so, Bergkamp, nicknamed the Ice Man by teammates, ever so coolly slotted the ball in the top corner past a stunned Kasey Keller.

It was a moment of genius from a product of the Ajax school. Bergkamp, who was to prove the strike was no fluke nine months later at the World Cup in France in the white heat of a quarter-final against Argentina in Marseille, celebrated in satisfaction rather than joy. It was the gratification of someone who was pleased with his goal, but it was also pride emanating from what was perceived to be a match-winning goal. It certainly deserved to be. Unfortunately, for him and Arsenal, it was not.

With nearly seven minutes added-on time, in what was to be their last attack, the Foxes won a corner. Parker crossed for Walsh to beat Vieira in the air. The ball then fell to Matt Prior, who was in space at the near post. Prior then nodded it back to Walsh, who had lost his man at the back post, and Martin O'Neil's captain headed into an empty net to the disbelief of Bergkamp, his teammates, Wenger and the travelling Gooners.

Despite the disappointment at two points dropped from a comfortable match-wining position, Bergkamp still rated the goal as one of his best ever saying,

> My favourite would be the hat-trick goal against Leicester because when you play football you have certain things in your mind which you want to achieve, and this was like that.
>
> In my mind I knew I wanted to do it like that and it worked exactly as I had planned it just two seconds before. With these sorts of goals there is a lot of skill involved and it has to come together.

Even Leicester manager Martin O'Neil had the decency to describe it as, 'one of the best goals I have ever seen'.

It was no surprise that *Match of the Day* viewers voted Bergkamp's hat-trick as their top three goals that month – for the first and only time.

There were no prizes for guessing which goal came first.

Bolton Wanderers (H)

13 September 1997

The following game after the incredible draw at Leicester brought another momentous occasion to the club.

Thirty-three-year-old Ian Wright, looking as lively and motivated as he did when entering League football as a twenty-one-year-old after receiving a succession of knock-backs from League clubs, scored his 179th goal for the Gunners against Bolton Wanderers, and in doing so broke the club goalscoring record that had stood since the club's first glory era in the 1930s, during a 4-1 rout at Highbury.

Arsène Wenger praised his forward's tremendous achievement, stating,

He is fantastic for the timing of his movement. It is so intelligent when he has not got the ball.

We had a bad start, we were 1-0 down, it could have made the team nervous but we were lucky to come quickly back and go into the lead very quickly. The image I would like to keep is the joy of the whole team when he broke the record, along the line when everyone came to congratulate him. It just shows that everybody in the team is concerned by it and that shows how well he's accepted by the whole team and how happy everybody was.

He's a quick thinker, a quick brain in the box, and he has the physical power to react. His second quality is that he's an explosive player, but he's very quiet and calm in front of goal at the right moment. And that's very rare.

And his third quality is mental: he wants it. He has the appetite. He has a huge appetite. That's the way champions are. They always want more. They want to go further. They're hungry.

All who were at Highbury that glorious afternoon would surely agree with Wenger's assessment of Ian Wright.

Arsenal: Seaman, Dixon, Bould, Grimandi, Winterburn, Petit, Vieira, Parlour, Overmars, Bergkamp, Wright. Substitutes: Platt for Parlour, Boa Morte for Overmars, Anelka for Wright. Not used: Marshall, Manninger.
Bolton Wanderers: Branagan, Frandsen, Taggart, Pollock, Sellars, Blake, Thompson, Bergsson, Beardsley, Phillips, McAnespie. Substitutions: Todd for McAnespie, Gunnlaugsson for Beardsley. Not used: Johansen, Ward, Taylor.
Referee: Neale Barry
Attendance: 38,138

Russell Thomas wrote in the Monday's *Guardian*:

> Arsène Wenger's spectacles misted with emotion as he led the applause for Arsenal's goal-record breaker. The manager had just witnessed confirmation in triplicate that goals – freakish or perfectly crafted – can change everything. They have certainly changed Ian Wright's life. In the autumn of his footballing career, Wright seems at his most vibrant. Age and disciplinary excesses cannot wither him. Natural fitness and robustness of spirit – quit apart from the gift of goals – made him the hat-trick hero of the hour, and, indelibly, Arsenal's record goalscorer.

A minute's silence was immaculately observed in memory of Diana, Princess of Wales, who died at the end of August, before Ian Wright finally broke Arsenal's all time goalscoring record with two goals in the space of three minutes during the first half against the visitors from the North West.

Yet Arsenal had been 1-0 down in the early stages of this momentous game, when the Wanderers' Alan Thompson put his recently promoted team ahead in the 14th minute, which, for a short while, threatened to spoil the party. Thompson succeeded in planting a header over 'keeper David Seaman who, while getting a hand onto the ball, failed to prevent it landing over the line.

While Wright was working to better his club tally of 177, his partner Dennis Bergkamp looked in fine fettle, hunting his seventh goal, including one for Holland in midweek.

In only the second minute, Bergkamp's vision sent Ray Parlour powering into the Bolton box as his shot appeared to take a deflection, before thudding back off the post. Wright followed up and looked certain to equal the record, but incredibly the ball rebounded off his shins when it seemed far easier to score, eventually going wide.

But Ian Wright finally equalled the North Londoners' striking record when he equalised in the 22nd minute, memorably twisting clear to collect the ball from Berkamp's perceptive pass before firing across 'keeper Branagan, who could not stop the ball from entering the far corner.

In a moment of unintended comedy, Wright celebrated by displaying a vest printed with the inscription '179 – Just done it' – even though his first goal had only equalled the legendary Cliff 'The Boy' Bastin's fifty-one-year record of 178 goals.

Once it was pointed out to Wright that he had merely drawn himself level with the 1930s Gunners icon, the effervescent South Londoner steeled himself for another try. In what was proof that it was his afternoon, Wright managed to officially break the record only 120 seconds later.

Wright's diagonal movement between the lines off the ball took him surging into a clutch of defenders, thus allowing Bergkamp safe passage into the Trotters' penalty area. Branagan then came out to close down the angle in blocking the Dutchman's drive, and as the ball looped away, Patrick Vieira took a swing at it before it fell to marksman Wright, who joyously slotted home from a yard with what had to be one of the easiest goals he had ever scored.

Cue pandemonium on the pitch and in the Highbury stands, which erupted with one of the loudest cheers the venerable old stadium had ever heard.

After the whole team had run to celebrate with the popular Wright, including David Seaman, Petit, who was proving to be an effective midfield partner for the burgeoning

Vieira, fed his colleague as he ran into the box, before the tall Frenchman picked out Wright at the back of the box.

Wright, proving he was human, and perhaps slightly distracted by the huge celebrations he had just led, fired his shot high into the side netting, spurning a chance of a hat-trick.

Yet, as the clock ticked into first-half injury time, the Gunners went 3-1 ahead when Bergkamp's run set up Parlour, whose powerful strike appeared to take a deflection off Phillips before slamming past Branagan and into the back of the net.

Typically, Wright went on to notch his hat-trick in the second half, as Arsène Wenger's team scored their fourth with nine minutes remaining as they ended up 4-1 winners.

His third was a perfect ending to a perfect afternoon that would be warmly remembered by all who witnessed it for many years to come – the day Ian Wright became an Arsenal legend and broke the club's all-time goalscoring record and reserved his place in Gunners history.

The man himself, speaking jubilantly of his premature record-breaking celebration after the game, exclaimed, 'I was actually happy before I put the ball in the net!'

So was every Arsenal fan at Highbury that wonderful, heart-warming afternoon.

Manchester United (A)

8 March 1998

In the first League match of 1998 on 10 January, Marc Overmars notched a double to help Arsenal to a win against Leeds United, led by ex-Arsenal manager George Graham. The canny Scot was in impish mode, returning to Highbury with bittersweet memories after twice wining the League, but also being removed from his position after allegations of illegal payments made by a Norwegian agent. After the defeat, Graham said,

> When you get a team like Arsenal who have got outstanding individuals, and you can keep them quiet for three quarters of the game, and all of a sudden one of them comes to life, that can win you the game.

Wenger chose to praise his player fulsomely saying,

> For me Overmars is a great player. Like many great players you expect always more than they produce. But you look at the players in the winger position in the midfield and you look at how many goals he's scored since the beginning of the season, and how important the goals were, who is the player in the English championship who's scored more goals than Overmars. He has great movement, he understands the game, he can run with the ball, he can work for the team. He has the speed.

Wenger's wise words on his flying winger were to be proved eerily accurate in the season, defining fixture at Old Trafford a few games later.

But first the team drew 2-2 at Coventry City. January ended with a 3-0 victory over Southampton at Highbury, all three goals coming in the space of seven minutes. A further two League wins in February, at home to Chelsea and Crystal Palace, pushed the Gunners into second spot, a huge nine points behind Manchester United, albeit having played two fewer games.

Yet a Manchester bookie, heady with hubris and no little arrogance, paid out all bets on Manchester United winning the League. His arrant contempt for the Gunners was not to be forgotten by the team or the fans in the crucial run-in.

However, as if to prove pride comes before a fall, to the bookie's satisfaction, Arsenal then dropped two points against West Ham United in early March, after a goalless stalemate in East London. A rare Christopher Wreh goal in the rescheduled match at Selhurst Park against the Crazy Gang of Wimbledon saw move Arsenal into second place – thereby setting up a title clash between the Londoners and Manchester United.

Alex Ferguson, ramping up the pressure on Arsenal said, 'It's getting tickly now – squeaky bum time I call it.'

In that intense early kick-off, Arsenal were to show they were more than equal to the pressure, with Marc Overmars also showing the wider footballing world that Wenger was a clairvoyant with his earlier appraisal of him and that ultimately the bookie from Manchester who paid out on United was foolish in betting against the Pride of London that year.

Man Utd: Schmeichel, G. Neville, Irwin, Berg, Curtis, Johnsen, Beckham, P. Neville, Scholes, Cole, Sheringham. Substitutes: Thornley for Curtis (52), Solskjaer for P. Neville (77), May for Johnsen. Not used: McClair, Van Der Gouw.
Arsenal: Manninger, Dixon, Adams, Keown, Winterburn, Vieira, Petit, Parlour, Overmars, Bergkamp, Wreh. Substitutes: Anelka for Wreh, Garde for Parlour (70). Not used: Hughes, Grimandi, Lukic.
Referee: Alan Wilkie
Attendance: 55,174

Paul Wilson writing in *The Guardian* in the aftermath of this match noted wryly,

> The bookmaker who has already paid out on Manchester United winning a fifth Premiership title was not expecting an Arsenal double, and ought to be wary of a double whammy between now and the end of the season.
>
> If any lucky punters who have collected early were watching this second – possibly crucial – home defeat, they must have been sorely tempted to invest a portion of their winnings on the Gunners finishing on top of the pile in May.
>
> The true significance of Marc Overmars's 80th-minute goal was not in cutting United's lead to six points, but in bringing about the defending champions' seventh league defeat. That is not normally a figure associated with successful title campaigns.

An early kick-off saw the race for the title move inexorably south, as Arsenal had looked like the League leaders at Old Trafford, not United.

Overmars had the game's first opportunity on 15 minutes. Collecting Bergkamp's pass, he skipped past Schmeichel, but went too wide to fire off a shot on target. He was then felled in the box by Curtis and was extremely unlucky not to be given a penalty as howls of protest came from the away end and 3,000 loyal travelling Gooners.

On the half-hour, Overmars ran past Curtis and Gary Neville, but only managed to strike the ball into the Dane's side netting. As if to emphasise their superiority, sixty seconds later Bergkmap nodded the ball to Ray Parlour, but with only the 'keeper to beat he shot well over.

Yet Overmars goal, when it came, fell in the midst of Arsenal's title-clinching run of ten League wins in a row. United, having ridden their luck for so long in the game, saw the Flying Dutchman Overmars run onto a flick from Anelka to slot a late goal past a despairing Schmeichel, causing an eruption of joy from his teammates and Arsenal fans present.

Overmars' surprise was only matched by Gary Neville's despair as the Red Devils' right-back had been given a torrid 90 minutes by the Londoners' Netherland international.

The win was to turn out to be a pivotal moment psychologically as much as points-wise.

The game was also notable for the cameras picking up on a couple of Gooners going absolutely mental in the away end. They, just like everyone else, knew the significance of this brave and impressive result from Wenger's men.

The Gunners' victory that day may have still rendered them six points off leaders United, but there were still two full months to play. The most important factor was that, for the first time, momentum and belief lay with Wenger's men – and the small detail of three games in hand on Ferguson's outfit. Arsenal were now in charge of their own destiny.

Another issue was the depth of resolve the legendary back four showed at Old Trafford. This match came in the midst of a spell of eight clean sheets in a row for Alex Manninger, deputising for the injured David Seaman.

Wenger said, 'We are a real team now, very solid, difficult to beat,' even if it was the Frenchman's turn to ramp up the pressure with mind games of his own by adding, 'United are still in the best position. Yet his final comment was the most revealing: 'But it's up to us now. It's in our hands for the first time.'

Alex Ferguson, on the other hand was at his archetypal best in handing out backhanded compliments laced with acidity. 'They deserved their victory,' he said before adding numerous caveats:

> But the circumstances were against us today. We started the game understrength and with a few players carrying injuries, and the midfield we finished up with was nothing like the shape of a true Manchester United midfield.
>
> I thought we were playing some decent football without ever looking like winning the match, but then we lost Johnsen and Phil Neville within minutes of each other and we couldn't regroup quickly enough to prevent them scoring.

In compiling those excuses, the Scot had inadvertently paid respect to Wenger's nous – a year after dismissing him in England, by saying 'He's a novice – he should keep his views to Japanese football'.

But as Ferguson concluded, 'It was a bad result for us. We now need to win seven matches in a row, which is something this club is capable of doing'.

With the way Wenger's Arsenal were playing in that glorious run-in, it really wouldn't have made a difference if they had.

Everton (H)

4 May 1998

In the title run-in, Alex Ferguson warned that it would be 'inevitable' that Arsenal would drop points. Yet they didn't. Two 1-0 wins, at home to Sheffield Wednesday, with an inspired performance from Petit and then Bolton Wanderers at the Reebok, from a terrific long distance Wreh strike, ensured the Gunners kept an eighth successive clean sheet, setting a new League record in the process.

Arsenal then beat Newcastle United 3-1, which included a glorious 30-yard strike form Vieira to ease within four points of Manchester United in early April. Bergkamp's reappearance after a three-match suspension helped Arsenal to trounce Blackburn Rovers 4-1 in the snow and sleet of Ewood Park over Easter. The team scorched Rovers off the park with three goals in the space of the opening 14 minutes, an inspired Anelka prominent. With United failing to claim victory over Newcastle, Arsenal led the table after trouncing Wimbledon 5-0 at Highbury.

A victory at Barnsley with a sublime piece of magic from Bergkamp and a vital 1-0 win four days later at home against Derby County resulted in Arsène Wenger's men requiring a single win from their remaining three games to clinch the League title.

The game against Everton was set up to make history – and history was duly made on an extraordinary afternoon in sunlit North London.

Arsenal: Seaman, Dixon, Winterburn, Vieira, Adams, Anelka, Overmars, Wreh, Keown, Parlour, Petit. Substitutes: Platt for Parlour, Wright for Anelka, Bould for Wreh. Not used: Manninger, Grimandi.
Everton: Myhre, Watson, Barmby, Ferguson, Hutchison, Short, Beagrie, Tiler, Ball, Bilic´, O'Kane. Substitutes: Madar for Beagrie, Oster for Billic, Farrelly for O'Kane. Not used: Gerrard, McCann.
Referee: Gerald Ashby
Attendance: 38,269

David Lacey in his *Guardian* match report noted,

In the end Arsenal passed the winning post without either breaking their stride or using the whip. An emphatic 4-0 win over Everton before an ecstatic crowd at Highbury confirmed their 11th Championship – and their first Premiership – and Arsène Wenger as the first foreign manager to lead a team to the English title.

They are worthy watchable champions. In a remarkably short space of time Wenger has achieved the ideal balance of defensive experience and attacking flair with, crucially, a mixture of athleticism and vision in midfield. At times the midfield pairing of Vieira and Petit has looked like four players in two given the amount of ground they cover.

Everton, stalked by relegation fears in a less than stellar vintage, were no match for Arsenal's vibrant attacking, intense pressing, superb movement and intelligent passing. Wenger's men fed off the crowd's anticipation and excitement as constant noise rolled around dear old Highbury. Arsenal overwhelmed the Merseysiders with their unrelenting, inexorable drive towards the title. Quite simply, the Gunners were uncontainable on that never-to-be-forgotten afternoon.

It was no surprise the first goal came after only five minutes on the stadium clock. Petit swung in a corner. Tony Adams, who had showed such courage not only on the pitch for Arsenal throughout his superb one club career but off it too in confronting his demons, pressured Slaven Bilic´ into heading into his own net.

On 28 minutes, Don Hutchison crunched into Petit. With the Arsenal staff fearing the worst, Overmars took the ball and, in driving forward, accelerated away from Everton's static back line, slotting the ball past 'keeper Thomas Myhre.

Now Highbury knew the end was nigh. Even Wenger, usually so calm, jumped into Pat Rice's arms as they both knew the title was coming back to Highbury after a gap of seven years.

Overmars then notched a second on 57 minutes to make the game safe, before a finale for the ages took place in front of disbelieving Arsenal eyes.

Steve Bould and Tony Adams, for so long derided by opposing fans and certain elements of the press as limited at best – cumbersome, slow and unimaginative at worst – contrived to produce a goal that was to leave everyone open mouthed at the sheer inventiveness and finesse of it.

Platt stopped a tired Everton run on the halfway line before Bould, finding himself in midfield, picked up the ball. His only thought was to play it forward to an onrushing colleague. Much to everyone's surprise, Tony Adams was the Arsenal man powering forward. Adams waited for the ball to bounce before chesting it down. The touch sent him to his left slightly, but the angle was not a problem as he pulled his left leg back, connecting perfectly on the half-volley to fire it into the net. His stupendous act sent Highbury into raptures at one of the most stirring goals the venerable old ground had ever – and would ever – witness.

Adams, in relief and surprise as much as celebration, simply stood with his arms extended in an iconic shot. An image that would later be carved into bronze outside a new state-of-the-art ground.

At that moment, Adams' attacking colleagues Ian Wright and Marc Overmars simply jumped on him in disbelief as the crowd erupted at what they had just seen – a real I was there moment.

It was also a goal that could only have been scored in a team led by Arsène Wenger, created and executed as it was by those two defensive colossuses who had previously been denied the chance to show attacking skills of their own. It truly was a magnificent goal on so many levels.

As the final whistle blew, Highbury staged a wonderful party. When the Arsenal fans, who took great pleasure in chanting long and loudly 'Wenger Wonderland', switched their vocal cords to 'Are You Watching Tottenham?', the mood was best summed up by the *Guardian's* Martin Thorpe, who wrote:

> Certainly the bedraggled arch rivals would have been looking on enviously. When Christian Gross held his first press conference at White Hart Lane he seemed a man out of his depth.
>
> When Wenger appeared at his, he appeared to be a man of depth. And so it has proved in the most victorious of ways.

Sue Quinn's feature on the post-match celebrations in and around the Highbury Barn pub encapsulated the day. The Barn, as it is known to all its regulars, is a watering hole renowned for its fiercely loyal and passionate Arsenal supporting locals who visit for pre and after game drinks. The report summed up what Wenger had brought to the club through the joyous nature of the festivities:

> At least a dozen of them had thrown themselves and their beer across the bonnet of the police car in utter jubilation, stopping it in its tracks, so even the cops inside had to smile. There was only one way to describe it. The place was going off.
>
> In Highbury Park outside the Highbury Barn pub, New Year's Eve and the Notting Hill Carnival had collided in a blur of red and white. Arsenal fans were 20 deep on the road and cars crawling back from the ground were doused with beer, jumped on and butted, but all those inside honked their horns as they celebrated the 4-0 victory over Everton that confirmed Arsenal as Premiership Champions ... inside the Barn was destruction. Those who had not secured a ticket for the game had watched victory happened on the television screens inside. The floor crunched underfoot with smashed glasses, torn up newspaper and red and white flags.
>
> As the evening wore on fans continued to straggle back from the game unable to pass through the swelling crowd outside the Barn, confronted by a barrier of fists in the air.

Meanwhile, an emotional Wenger spoke to the press amid the joyous celebrations on and off the pitch after the Premiership trophy had been lifted by Tony Adams. A packed Highbury and perfect late afternoon blue sky acted as a perfect backdrop. He said, 'Maybe it's the biggest satisfaction in my career until now. 'I'm very happy because we had a combination of exciting, entertaining football and efficiency.'

Even Alex Ferguson had to tip his hat to the new Champions of England. He said,

> In the home stretch, they had put together a sequence of ten straight victories and only a truly special team could do that in a league as tough as ours.
>
> They had notable quality in every department and Arsène Wenger deserves immense credit for integrating his English and foreign players into such a cohesive, powerful and highly motivated unit.

The last word deservedly went to Wenger and his astounding achievement fewer than eighteen months since he arrived to *Evening Standard* billboards proclaiming 'Arsène Who?' Yet even Wenger conceded he wasn't sure that his team his could it from a staggering thirteen points behind United.

> Yes I really thought we couldn't win it then. Of course I didn't say it but I thought even a Champions League place was beyond us.
>
> I'm proud to be the first foreign manager to win the championship. I know how difficult it is to win. This is one way for me to repay the confidence that directors had in me because they were brave against what people thought.

And with big grin on his face he added, 'I am going out tonight to dinner and having a good French wine.'

If anyone deserved a decent drink after the heroics, not only of the day that will live forever in Arsenal memories but of a staggering season in which his team had shown all their qualities, it was Arsène Wenger.

Newcastle United (N)

16 May 1998

Two insipid League defeats followed that never-to-be-forgotten Premier League, clinching match against Everton at Highbury – 4-0 at Anfield three days later where the players looked as if they were still in celebratory mode and a 1-0 defeat at a packed Villa Park. The loss was notable for Dwight York's cheeky 'Panenka' style penalty, which fooled an embarrassed David Seaman who failed to anticipate the ball being dinked chest height through the middle of his goal. The game would also prove to be goal scoring legend Ian Wright's last-ever game for the club.

Yet the two League defeats simply didn't matter in the scheme of things. What did matter was the Gunners aiming to win the FA Cup final to complete only the second double in the club's long and illustrious history. They were up against against a Kenny Dalglish led Newcastle United side, who had reached their first final since an uncomfortable 3-0 defeat by Bill Shankly's Liverpool in 1974.

Arsenal had commenced their campaign with a feeble 0-0 draw at home to Port Vale. The replay in the Potteries saw the North Londoners win on penalties 4-3. Dennis Bergkamp struck from outside the area – a nonchalant strike that dipped over Valiants 'keeper Musselwhite in the 100th minute to enter the right-hand side of his net, much to the joy of the travelling contingent. However, the home team lived up to their nickname as Corden equalised two minutes from the end of extra time to send the tie to penalties. A leveller that had the rest of the country licking their lips in anticipation of a Cup giant-killing and Wenger's second FA Cup defeat in four matches. The fraught matter of a penalty shoot-out was successfully navigated in favour of the visitors in dramatic fashion. Port Vale full-back Allen Tankard in the last of his team's five scheduled spot-kicks blasted the ball high over the bar, allowing the Gunners to win 4-3 on penalties.

Marc Overmars and Ray Parlour made sure a potentially tricky trip to second tier Middlesbrough in round four was negotiated safely in a 2-1 win. 'This was the game that taught me about the passion of the FA Cup,' Wenger said later. The game was made noteworthy by the superb response by the travelling Arsenal fans to 'Boro player and Arsenal legend Paul Merson. The Northolt-born forward and cried when Wenger, in an unexpected move at the end of the 1996/97 Premiership season, sold him to the relegated Teeside outfit in a £5 million deal – making him the most expensive player ever signed by a non-Premiership club and forever leaving him stranded on ninety-nine goals in all competitions.

Crystal Palace were overcome 2-1 with goals from Anelka and Bergkamp at Selhurst Park after another drab 0-0 at Highbury. West Ham were the Gunners' sixth-round scalp, winning 4-3 on penalties at Upton Park after a 1-1 draw in North London. The replay was a feisty affair, with Bergkamp being sent off for elbowing Steve Lomas in the face after 35 minutes. Anelka scored with a well-taken goal just before half-time, but another ex-Arsenal man John Hartson squeezed a shot past the Austrian 'keeper Alex Manninger, who was ably standing in for the injured David Seaman with five minutes to go. Abou for the Irons struck the final spot-kick against the post as the 4,000 Gooners in the Boleyn Ground erupted with relief as much as joy. A rare Christopher Wreh goal clinched a 1-0 win over Wolves in the Villa Park semi-final, meaning Arsenal were back at Wembley for an FA Cup final for the first time in five years.

Arsenal: Seaman, Dixon, Adams (c), Keown, Winterburn, Parlour, Vieira, Petit, Overmars, Wreh, Anelka. Substitutes: Platt for Wreh. Not used: Manninger, Bould, Grimandi, Wright.
Newcastle United: Given, Barton, Howey, Dabizas, Pearce, Lee (c), Batty, Speed, Pistone, Ketsbaia, Shearer. Substitutes: Andersson for Pearce, Watson for Barton, Barnes for Ketsbaia. Not used: Hislop, Albert.
Score: 2-0
Attendance: 79,183

Saturday 16 May 1998 is a date forever etched in the consciousness of Arsenal fans everywhere. It was the day the Gunners clinched their second double in the club's history, and their first such achievement since 1971. Even the weather made an effort as the near heatwave temperatures saw a cloudless sky, which was more reminiscent of archetypical Cup final weather – even if such meteorological conditions are far more common in the mind's eye and wistful memories than in reality.

Arsène Wenger brought a Gallic touch of *elan* to the traditional team suits, opting to choose for black shirts. Although, he stated categorically that he did not have a say in the equally as traditional Cup final song. A jaunty number entitled 'Hot Stuff' by Arsenal FC eventually reached the giddy heights of number nine, adapted from the original 1979 Donna Summer song. 'Started off the season nothing stopped us/everything was going Wright, Wright, Wright.' To Arsenal fans of a certain vintage. the song still brings back happy memories of the time, and certainly when the video is viewed, which, among the requisite clips of cracking goals from the season, was interspersed with the lads mucking around with headphones on while attempting to sing the chorus.

However, there was to be no frivolity at the kick-off.

After a scrappy opening, the North Londoners took charge when Ray Parlour delivered an inch-perfect cross for nineteen-year-old Nicholas Anelka, who saw the ball sail agonisingly over the bar, with Shay Given beaten.

The deadlock wasn't to last long. Overmars stormed onto a long pass from Emmanuel Petit, his pace scorching past Alessandro Piston before he toe-poked the ball through the overworked Given's legs to send half of Wembley into joyous celebration.

The Dutch winger's goal was his sixteenth of a memorable season. The game was far less memorable for the old warhorse Stuart Pearce who played on despite receiving a head wound early on. The England captain bound for the 1998 France World Cup experienced a disheartening afternoon as he and fellow strike partner Temuri Ketsbaia were starved of service as the twin red-and-white French pillars *dans la milleu de terrain* Vieria and Petit won every ball.

Newcastle, to their credit, pushed forward after the half-time but were denied by the woodwork twice. Nikos Dabizas' 62nd minute header clipped the top of the bar. Two minutes later, Shearer seized on a rare Martin Keown error, but his drilled left-foot shot hit the inside of a post, with Seaman beaten. Soon after, the North Easterner's brief assault was over when Anelka escaped the offside trap, used his youthful strength and power to hold off Steve Howey before firing past Given to make it 2-0. In doing so, he became the third youngest player to score in a final. More importantly, goal number two quelled any thought of a Newcastle revival and completely deflated their ambitions as the sun beat down relentlessly.

Man of the match, the tireless Ray Parlour was a constant menace to the Magpies, his industry never allowing them a second to settle. But in truth, all eleven Arsenal players were exceptional against a Newcastle side who did not do themselves justice on a hot day.

The *Daily Mirror*'s player ratings did not hold back, stating the Geordie captain Alan Shearer endured a 'hot, miserable, frustrating afternoon', adding, 'Shearer got so frustrated by it all that he clumsily and brazenly fouled Adams, but he must get some credit for being big enough to apologise for his actions immediately afterwards.'

They also slammed Italian Alessandro Pistone saying,

The first Arsenal goal, so brilliantly and speedily executed by Overmars, settled this contest early on. If it was a fight, the ref would have been forced to stop it. Pistone never looked comfortable when confronted by the livewire Dutchman and Overmars spent the rest of the game threatening a repeat performance to make it a thoroughly miserable day for the outclassed and outrun Italian defender.

Sportingly, the Newcastle fans applauded the Arsenal team as they made their way up the Wembley steps to collect the trophy as Arsenal fans celebrated the double.

Arsène Wenger and Tony Adams were captured in an iconic father/son looking photograph, with the Frenchman placing his hand tenderly on Adam's neck and the centre-half looking at him in reverence in a remarkable display of mutual respect.

When the Frenchman was asked what he said to his loyal captain on the pitch he replied, 'I told Tony I was proud of him and that he should be proud of himself.'

With Tony Adams and the rest of the squad now firm believers in Wenger methods, there would be a lot more success to come. But this day at Wembley will always be remembered as the FA Cup final win that clinched Arsenal their second double and a place in history.

Manchester United (N)

14 April 1999

The 1998/99 season started brightly, and with such high hopes after Arsenal clinched the double the year before in Arsène Wenger's first full season in charge.

The Charity Shield was won in convincing fashion against the previous season's Premiership runners-up Manchester United, with goals from Marc Overmars, Christopher Wreh and Nicolas Anelka. In unusual statistics, it was the first time a southern team had won the shield outright since 1962, and was the Red Devils first loss in Wembley's traditional curtain-raiser in seven matches.

Arsenal then repeated the same scoreline against Alex Ferguson's team a month later at Highbury in the League. The *Daily Mirror* wrote of Gunners debutant Freddie Ljungberg,

LJUNBERG THE PUNK ROCKS UNITED
Anarchy reigned at Highbury as Arsenal shredded Manchester United an acclaimed a new hero – Sid Vicious. Ljungberg, named after the Sex Pistols punk rocker because of his spiky hairdo, made his debut a day to remember.

Wenger added of the comprehensive League victory over his rivals, which boded well for trophies that year: 'That is probably as good as it gets, definitely our best for some time. We had our offensive power back. I was pleased with this victory.'

In their Cup run, Arsenal had beaten Preston North End 4-2 at Deepdale (Boa Morte, Petit (2), Overmars), triumphed 2-1 at Wolves (Overmars, Bergkamp), and beat Sheffield United 2-1, after Wenger graciously allowed the first game to be replayed, when Kanu scored a goal after breaking an unwritten convention by harrying a throw-in back to the visitors after an injury. The Sheffield United manager at the time, Steve Bruce, showed little grace or gave Wenger little credit, and moaned that the game should have been played at Bramall Lane. As it was, Arsenal repeated the scoreline easily and then eased past Derby County in the quarter-final, with a last-minute goal by Kanu in a 1-0.

The original semi-final at Villa Park ended in a 0-0 stalemate, with both teams cancelling each other out. Nelson Vivas was sent off for the Gunners, which set up the reply at the same venue just three days later. It was to be the last year of FA Cup replays due to the ever-increasing schedule of top level football in England.

After the best two teams in England clashed in what would an unforgettable match.

It was a defining fixture for Wenger – not only for what they could have won but the energising effect it had on the victors. It was hugely disappointing that the victors were not from London.

Arsenal: Seaman, Dixon, Winterburn, Keown, Adams, Vieira, Petit, Parlour, Ljungberg, Bergkamp, Anelka. Substitutes: Overmars for Ljungberg (62), Kanu for Parlour, Bould for Petit. Not used: Vivas, Lukic.

Manchester United: Schmeichel, P. Neville, Johnsen, G. Neville, Stam, Beckham, Butt, Keane, Blomqvist, Sheringham, Solskjaer. Substitutes: Giggs for Blomqvist, Yorke for Solskjaer, Scholes for Sheringham (76). Not used: Irwin, van der Gouw.

Referee: David Elleray

Attendance: 30,223

This was a game that will be talked about as long as people talk about the FA Cup. It had everything: great goals, a sending off, a last-minute missed penalty, teak-tough midfield battles, great techniques and a bitter rivalry. It was as exciting a match as anyone could wish to see between the two undisputed giants of English football at the time.

David Beckham played a clever one-two with the man all Gooners loved to hate, Teddy Sheringham, before curling a precise shot past David Seaman's despairing dive and into the net from 25 yards.

Harrow schoolmaster Ellerary then booked four players in seven minutes. With just 21 minutes to go until the end of normal time, Bergkamp fired a shot that took a substantial deflection off Jaap Stam, finishing beyond their big Danish goalkeeper and into the net to level the scores at 1-1.

Four minutes later, the combustible Keane was sent off in the 74th minute after a second yellow for an ill-judged lunge on Overmars, who had by then substituted Ljungberg.

As Arsenal stepped up the pressure, something had to give. In injury time, Ray Parlour dribbled into the box, more on instinct than anything else – as like many players on both sides who had given their all in two titanic battles, he looked spent. Yet so was Phil Neville, who made a tired attempt to stop him as he cut inside him. Elleray pointed to the spot and, with fewer than sixty seconds remaining, Dennis Bergkamp stepped up to take the penalty that could take Arsenal to Wembley.

The spot-kick was of such vital importance to both teams. Obviously, if he scored it would invariably result in Arsenal going through to the Cup final for the second year in a row under Wenger. But also in psychological terms, if Wenger's men could beat United, the damage done to their morale could have been incalculable in terms of the League title challenge – not to mention their Champions League hopes.

The ground stilled as every one of the spectators present knew the importance of the moment. Bergkamp, who had missed the previous year's final through injury, ran towards the ball. Schmeichel, also aware of the importance, looked loose-limbed and far more relaxed than a rapidly tensing Bergkamp. knowing that goalkeepers in penalty situations have nothing to lose, The Dutchman connected beautifully with the ball and hit it firmly, low to the 'keeper's right – but Schmeichel had guessed correctly and saved it. To the groans and utter despair of all Arsenal fans present, not to mention a hopelessly despondent Bergkamp, Elleray blew shortly afterwards. On such moments, titles, trophies and silverware are decided.

United, galvanised by the miss looked the stronger in extra time. And so it was that the Red Devils took the lead when Giggs intercepted a tired cross-field pass from Vieira on 109 minutes and proceeded to run through an exhausted Gunners defence. Such was their fatigue they failed to put in a challenge that would normally deprive substitute Giggs, far fresher than his rivals, of the ball. And so Giggs simply carried on running through the Arsenal defence until he found the time and space to fire the ball into the roof of the net past Seaman – who perhaps should have stood up a fraction longer.

Giggs then reflected the intensity of the match by losing all inhibitions, running along the touchline bare-chested after flinging his top off in celebration to reveal a surprisingly hirsute torso. It was all too much for stunned Arsenal fans, and nine minutes later Elleray blew the whistle, confirming United the victors. United were off to Wembley while Wenger had to pick his men up off the floor.

He said afterwards, looking as dejected as anyone had seen him:

> It is not east to take a defeat such as this. But what you can demand of your team is that they give everything. They are very sad today of course because it was not our night at all and we were really, I think unlucky. The two team teams are very close to each other. It was a smashing game, and in the end the luckiest won. We had the chances to win. Especially we had the penalty with a minute to go. So you expect, of course, to win the game. But that's football.
>
> We were a little bit unlucky, lost the ball in the middle of the park and Giggs did the rest. There were one or two rebounds for him, but Giggs is a great player. It was a fantastic goal. They have so many qualities in the middle of the park and up front every ball you lose is dangerous.
>
> But there's no reproach. I would like to congratulate my team. They were fantastic. They are very sad tonight. They have shown again they are a great team. Sometimes you can say that when you lose.

Manchester United manager Alex Ferguson typically begged to differ from Wenger's viewpoint and insisted, 'I think we deserved the win. Over the two legs I think we were the better team. The players have played in agony to get the victory. Ryan Giggs had injured himself near the end also.'

Sky's Martin Tyler, talking to Arsenal journalist Myles Palmer and quoted in his book, *The Professor: Arsène Wenger,* said,

> Arsenal had the Indian sign on United until Dennis Bergkamp's penalty was saved by Schmeichel. I've never seen Wenger more angry after a game than that night. Not just losing the Cup, but losing that edge that they had over Manchester United. They'd had a very good recent record and they beat them again the Charity Shield. The general feeling around at the time was the best Arsenal would beat the best Manchester United. That seems an extraordinary thing to say now. But through 1998 and 1999 that was what many people believed – if Arsenal got their best team out, which they didn't always do.

What is somewhat forgotten in the juddering aftershocks of the game is that Ryan Giggs was at the peak of his game and career and that the goal he scored that night against a very tired Gunners backline – was one of the best goals ever struck in FA Cup football.

There was no dishonour for Wenger and his brave boys to lose the semi-final replay night. Immense disappointment, yes, dishonour no.

But what would it mean in terms of the race for the title?

Leeds United (A)

11 May 1999

Wenger, in trying to pick his men up in the League title run-in after the devastating defeat by Manchester United in the FA Cup semi-final replay said,

It's part of our job. We want to win, and if you want to win, you have of course to survive disappointments. And we have to show that in the remaining games that we can react. When you lose of course you're very sad. But at the moment, it's history. We just have to look forward.

Displaying true character, the loss was shrugged off the following Monday as Arsenal annihilated Wimbledon 5-1 at a subdued Highbury. The Gunners then travelled to Teeside to hand Middlesbrough the mother of all beatings – 6-1 on their home turf – before prevailing against Derby County 1-0 in a tense game in London. The scene was set for a vital North London derby, but Arsenal again showed their class, desire and – in terms of the growing gap in class between them and Spurs – utter disdain by engulfing them 3-1 at White Hart Lane, including a memorable virtuoso strike from Kanu.

The Lilywhites' manager on the night was a certain George Graham. It must have warmed Arsenal fans hearts to hear him speak glowingly of the team that had handed his side a footballing lesson saying, 'Arsenal, especially in the first half were outstanding. On the break they were real quality tonight.'

Wenger commented on another comprehensive victory in the North London derby: 'Our passing was excellent, our runs were great, and every time we got through the first defending of Tottenham we were dangerous.'

Yet when asked what he thought would happen with two games to go with United and Arsenal neck and neck in an absorbing title race, Wenger replied, a little hesitantly, 'I don't know. It's difficult to predict who will win it, and how they will win it.'

Little did he know it would be another defining defeat that would ultimately hand the trophy to United.

Going in to the game, Leeds United boss and Arsenal's record appearance maker David O'Leary warned Arsenal not to expect any favours. That was fair enough – everyone knows in football that you don't expect (or want) favours from anyone. What you do expect, however, certainly from the man who has made more appearances than anyone else on the planet for your club, is to show a little respect to the present incumbent.

However, O'Leary, before engaging his brain, said provocatively,

Wenger has a lot of old defenders there [including ones O'Leary himself battled alongside with in the trenches] and there is a risk that they will all go at the same time. People say it's half the team, but for me it's more than that. Replacing them is going to be a big job and a long job and it may be that Arsène won't want the challenge of it.

It's going to be some night. This will be a great way to finish off our home programme and we shall be going all out to beat them. It won't be difficult for me, trying to beat my old club, even when I know there is so much at stake for them, because it's almost five years since I left Highbury and a lot of things have changed there in the meantime.

A lot of things had changed at Arsenal – what O'Leary had omitted to say was that it had all changed for the better and his disrespectful words about the club and Wenger were not to be forgotten by Arsenal fans with long memories. Nor would his over the top celebrations on the Elland Road pitch be forgotten either, or the fact that he was to last less than another year in the job.

But that pivotal night showed something had to give in the race for the title between United and Arsenal, and for the second time in less than a month it was a Gunners side that ultimately yielded, resulting, disastrously, in a further loss of silverware.

Leeds United: Martyn, Woodgate, Radebe, Harte, Haaland, Bowyer, Batty, Hopkin, Kewell, Smith, Hasselbaink.
Arsenal: Seaman, Dixon, Adams, Keown, Winterburn, Parlour, Petit, Vieira, Overmars, Anelka, Bergkamp. Substitutes: Vivas for Winterburn, Diawara for Parlour, Kanu for Overmars.
Referee: Gary Willard
Attendance: 40,124

Oliver Holt wrote in his *Times* match report after the game:

Somewhere, sometime, something had to give. Manchester United and Arsenal have been going at each other for months, refusing to bow, refusing to yield, until it seemed that neither would submit, that they would have to be fragged apart by goal difference. Last night, worn out by the chase, Arsenal finally caved in.

There was irony bordering on perversity in the fact that it should be at Elland Road, the home of the supporters who love to hate Manchester United, where the title race appeared to swing decisively away from the champions towards Alex Ferguson's side.

Arsenal had suffered a crushing defeat – their first since December. Leeds played like men possessed, which was a shame as under O'Leary they had more often than not shown little appetite for digging deep that season. The evening against Arsenal was different. The truculent Lee Bowyer played well in hounding and tacking an Arsenal midfield that was running on instinct rather than energy. Defender Lucas Radebe showed resolution and David Batty industriousness. Indeed, he almost scored after fifty seconds as he picked up a rebound by David Hopkin, volleying just over Seaman's head and the bar.

Wenger said later that his team were too tired to replicate their normal energy levels, but Bergkamp, his team's best player on the night, made Martyn work in keeping out a right-footed curler.

The Dutchman nearly carved another chance out of nothing in the second half, when he ran through a well-peopled Leeds box only to see his drive agonisingly cleared off the line by Radebe and a second bite at the cherry cleared by the efforts of Martyn and Radebe again.

Adams was then infuriated by something that a snarling Alan Smith said to him. Smith, who was to later desert Elland Road for hated rivals Manchester United, allegedly made an uncalled for comment about Adams' alcoholism. The power of the juddering tackle Arsenal's defensive legend made on Smith next time the two came into contact was felt by the club's 3,000 travelling fans – one of which was the author – before being roundly applauded for its intensity, showing solidarity for a clearly rattled Adams, who was normally so unflappable on the pitch.

Matt Dickinson added of the moment in *The Times*, 'When even the Arsenal captain was swept away in the maelstrom, it was proof enough that Arsène Wenger's side had lost their mast, rudder, and were heading for the rocks.'

But with five minutes remaining, Jimmy Floyd Hasselbaink, who had scored every time he had played Arsenal in his career up until then, continued the record. He powered a diving header past Seaman and into the net to hand Leeds a 1-0 win that was to spell the end of Arsenal's title hopes. Mathematically, it was still possible despite the defeat, but with Spurs going to Old Trafford on the last day of the season no one envisaged anything other than an easy United win – which turned out to be the case.

At Elland Road, after Arsenal's shattering 1-0 defeat, a graceless O'Leary mouthed, 'I haven't got any sympathy for them. You win the championship by doing it off your own back.'

A devastated Wenger said, 'We are disappointed. We gave everything,' before taking into account O'Leary's comments by stating sardonically, 'I know Leeds are supposed to hate Manchester United but maybe they hate us more.'

Manchester United went on to win the League by one point from Arsenal that year. They also beat Newcastle United 2-0 in the 1999 FA Cup final. Despite being 1-0 down to Bayern Munich in the Champions League final in the Nou Camp, they improbably triumphed 2-1, leaving Ferguson to utter that immortal line: 'Football, bloody hell.'

For Arsène Wenger, his team and Gooners everywhere, it could have all been so different had they not lost to United in the FA Cup semi-final replay – and at Elland Road to a charmless David O'Leary.

Not only would victories in both allowed Arsenal to potentially lift a second double in two seasons, but with United suffering a conceivable loss of momentum, it is debatable whether they would even have triumphed in Spain.

The reality – and one needing to be acknowledged as all that truly counts is the record books left Arsenal empty handed. Despite a heroic effort on all fronts from one of the best teams in their history.

Football, bloody hell.

11

Chelsea (A)

23 October 1999

In a home game against Watford a month earlier, in which a late Kanu strike gave the Gunners all three points, it was instructive when Wenger said, 'If you keep scoring late, you believe you can score late.'

Gunners' fans, enthused by another good start to the season, followed Arsenal out to Barcelona in large numbers a week after the Watford game to see their team gain a creditable draw 1-1 in the Nou Camp. A contentious game at Upton Park soon after saw Patrick Vieira receive a lengthy ban for spitting at Neil Ruddock. While Vieira should never have done what he did, Ruddock was unacceptably crass in alleging afterwards that hecould 'smell the garlic on his breath', yet his inflammatory comments were shamefully ignored by the FA.

Arsenal then eased past Everton 4-1 before taking on Barcelona at Wembley. In a valiant performance in front of a capacity 73,000 crowd, they were undone by the sheer moments of genius by the Catalans, which featured a certain Pep Guardiola in midfield as they triumphed 4-2. It was a performance that prompted Matt Dickinson of *The Times* to note,

> They tried, how they tried, but they were ultimately given a lesson in the art of the counter attack by a Barcelona side who are better equipped than any in the world at picking defences apart ... blink and you missed something.

It was a description that could well have applied to the following Saturday's game at Stamford Bridge, in which Nigerian Nwankwo Kanu scored one of the greatest hat-tricks in the club's history.

Chelsea: De Goey, Ferrer, Desailly, Leboeuf, Babayaro, Petrescu, Wise, Deschamps, Le Saux, Sutton, Flo. Substitutes: Hogh, Poyet, Morris, Cudicini, Zola.
Arsenal: Seaman, Dixon, Keown, Adams, Silvinho, Parlour, Ljungberg, Petit, Overmars, Kanu, Suker. Substitutes: Vivas, Manninger, Henry, Upson, Vernazza.
Referee: Alan Wilkie
Attendance: 34,958

With forty-nine yellow cards handed out in the last seven meetings between the two sides, it was fair to state that the biggest North *v.* West London match up the capital had to offer was invariably a tasty display of aggression. This match was no different, with Lee Dixon receiving a yellow for a late foul on Graeme Le Saux with fewer than 180 seconds on the clock. Perhaps it was a coincidence, although the two of them shared an antagonistic history as they were both sent off for tangling a year earlier.

This match was shorn of its two most creative protagonists through injury – Zola and Bergkamp – with the Arsenal man picking up a strain in the defeat to Barcelona at Wembley days earlier. Their collective absences ensured play would be hectic rather than refined, with the game likely to be settled with a flash of inspiration not perspiration.

And so it proved.

The weather was ultimately to assist Arsenal's cause, pouring down intermittently thereby creating conditions where the ball would stick to the greasy surface. It was to be an environment in which one of Wenger's men would capitalise late on in the game. But only after Chelsea went 2-0 up to the premature joy of their gloating support.

Blues striker Tore Andre Flo gave the Stamford Bridge outfit a lead on 39 minutes as he jumped above the normally proficient Gunners defence to nod Dan Petrescu's cross that evaded David Seaman.

Six minutes after the restart, the North London giants found themselves two goals behind, with the Romanian Petrescu this time being the scorer rather than creator – he surprisingly leapt above Wenger's defence to head home his team's second from a Le Saux cross.

Yet Arsenal began to show the character they were famed for. As the rain lashed down in stair rods, rapidly turning the Stamford Bridge pitch into a sodden mess, Arsenal stepped up their intent, if not their end product. With only 15 minutes remaining and the score still 2-0, Kanu took a Marc Overmars drive that was petering out before poking it into the net with just enough momentum to push it past De Goey.

Kanu, a cult figure at Arsenal for his close control and sure technique, honed in the dusty games of street football he played as a child in his Nigerian hometown of Owerri, then drew Wenger's team level with just five minutes left.

The Uruguayan Gus Poyet struggled to reach an Overmars cross and missed completely. This granted Kanu the time and liberty to coolly push the ball into open space before driving the ball past a surprised De Goey at his near post.

The 3,000 travelling Gooners watching at that corner along the touchline went berserk in celebration. But judging by their team's reaction, it was clear they believed there was still unfinished business in this hard-fought London derby.

The momentum was well and truly with Wenger's men now – and Chelsea knew it. Like a boxer clinging on desperately in the hope of hearing the bell, Chelsea now struggled to cope with the rampant Gunners.

As the clock ticked into injury time, Kanu showed the class that had won him a Champions League winners' medal as a talented teenager in Ajax's acclaimed side of the mid-1990s. What happened next was one of the most joyful and unexpected moments in Arsenal's history.

Davor Suker, working tirelessly for his team, licked up a ball in the centre of the park before playing it out wide. Unfortunately, he looked to have overhit his wide pass for Kanu to run onto to the left flank. Yet because of the sodden surface, the ball held up, forcing a Chelsea defender to clear his lines.

However, despite the heavy pitch, Kanu, with a spring in his step that only comes from scoring two late goals, chased down the attempted clearance and blocked it in the 90th minute. The ball, which could have gone anywhere, flew down the line. On a normal day, it would have gone off for a goal kick, but with the pitch saturated, it held up on the edge of the area near the goal line, allowing Kanu to run onto it.

There would have been no danger still, had De Goey not had a rush of blood that afflicts all goalkeepers from time to time. Perhaps in an effort to atone for his previous error, the tall 'keeper came rushing off his line, ostensibly to tackle Arsenal's erstwhile Nigerian, or at the very least block the ball. Kanu, sensing the onrushing De Goey, opened up his body to deceive the 'keeper into thinking he would angle the ball into the crowded box in the hope that one of his teammates could reach it.

What he did next was a work of art.

With De Goey committed to an injudicious tackle, Kanu then swerved his body to take the ball past the foolish 'keeper in one decisive moment. With his man beaten and the ball trickling along the byline, Kanu looked up to see an open net and lifted the ball into the net despite a clutch of blue shirts in the box and Frank Leboeuf on the goal line. As the Chelsea players look shocked and dejected at such impudence, Kanu ran towards the celebrating Arsenal fans, of which I was one, who could barely believe what they had witnessed.

Moments later, the whistle blew, and Arsenal not only achieved an important victory over their rivals – London ones to boot – but those present saw a late hat-trick that will live forever in the memory.

As Wenger said a few weeks previously, 'If you keep scoring late, you believe you can score late.'

12

Galatasaray (N)

17 May 2000

The crushing 4-2 Champions League defeat by Barcelona at Wembley on matchday four saw their hopes of finishing top of Group B ended by the comprehensive reverse. But it was the 1-0 home loss to a Gabriel Batistuta stunner in the next round of matches that effectively put paid to the Gunners' realistic chance of qualifying from the group at all. An entertaining 3-2 victory away to AIK Solna in the Rasunda Stadium in Stockholm on matchday six may have cheered the 500 travelling fans, including the author, to Sweden's capital, but despite the three points, Arsenal finished third, a point behind the Italians. The placing would mean staying in Europe, but to compete in the far less prestigious (and far less financially rewarding) UEFA Cup.

Nevertheless, Wenger approached their task with a seriousness that belied their disappointment at exiting Europe's premier trophy by picking a full strength side in their first UEFA Cup tie. In the event, they comfortably beat Nantes 3-0 at Highbury with Bergkamp netting, Overmars scoring with a penalty, and Nigel Winterburn hitting a rare goal for the club to render the second leg a formality. The lack of pressure resulted in an open game that ended 3-3 on France's Atlantic coast as Overmars struck again, along with Henry and Gilles Grimandi. The 6-3 aggregate victory propelled Wenger's men into a trip to Northern Spain to play Deportivo La Coruna. A memorable 5-1 victory in North London saw Henry hit two, with Bergkamp, Kanu and Lee Dixon supplementing the score, rending the second leg in Galicia a formality, even if it ended in a 2-1 defeat (Henry). However, the result would not deter manager Javier Irureta's men from claiming their first league title since they were founded in 1906, a fact that made Arsenal's evisceration of La Coruna at Highbury even more impressive.

The Germans of Werder Bremen were beaten 2-0 (Henry, Ljungberg) at fortress Highbury, with the move back after their Wembley sojourn agreeing with the North Londoners. An improbable Ray Parlour hat-trick at the Weserstadion in north-west Germany, along with another Henry strike saw the Londoners move effortlessly into the last four.

A tense first-leg semi-final at Highbury saw Arsenal edge the match 1-0 (Bergkamp) against the *Les Sang et Or* (Blood and Gold) of Lens from Northern France. A 2-1 win at the Stade Bollaert-Delelis, with Henry and Kanu strikes, ensured Arsenal's 1999/2000 European adventure would result in reaching the final of a tournament that hadn't even been entered into at the start of a long season. But now they had reached the UEFA Cup final in Copenhagen – the scene of their unforgettable backs to the wall victory over a star-studded Parma team six years previously – they were determined to win it. Only Galatasaray stood between them and glory.

Arsenal: Seaman, Dixon, Keown, Adams (c), Sylvinho, Parlour, Petit, Vieira, Overmars, Bergkamp, Henry. Substitutes: Kanu for Bergkamp, Suker for Overmars. Not used: Lukic, Winterburn, Luzhny, Grimandi, Malz.

Galatasaray: Taffarel, Capone, Korkmaz (c), Popescu, Penbe, Davala, Kaya, Hagi, Buruk, Erdem, Şükür. Substitutes: Unsal for Buruk, Yildirim for Kaya, Sas for Erdem. Not used: Akyel, Yozgatlı, Márcio.

Score: 0-0 aet, Galatasaray won 4-1 on penalties.

Attendance: 38,919

Unfortunately, Copenhagen in 2000 for Arsenal fans would be remembered far less fondly than the last time they played in a European final in the Danish capital. The match would be forever remembered for off-field events, which saw the day labelled as the Battle of Copenhagen. City Hall Square in the centre of the city, a place where over 20,000 Gooners partied peaceably before and after the Cup Winners' Cup final, was now the setting for a series of violent clashes between supporters of Arsenal and Turkish fans of Galatasaray. Four people were stabbed, nineteen injured and sixty arrested as firms of hooligans from other British clubs joined together in the trouble, which was in direct response to the murder of two Leeds United fans in Istanbul ahead of their semi-final against the Turkish side. Despite local police deploying 2,000 officers to the square and surrounding environs, as well as being warned of potential trouble in the lead up to the match by British Football Intelligence, violence, tear gas and an all-pervading, ugly atmosphere marred what should have been a showcase final.

The game itself was full of missed chances with Thierry Henry having a number of terrific strikes saved by Gala's Brazilian 'keeper Claudio Taffarel, along with Overmars who saw a shot fly narrowly wide. In the second period of extra time, Henry was prevented a winner when Taffarel stopped his powerful header as Arsenal dominated but agonisingly failed to score – itself a continuation of the first 90 minutes. However, it wasn't all one-way traffic, as midfielder Arif Erdem beat the offside trap yet pulled his strike wide during a one-on-one with Seaman. But perhaps the easiest chance fell to Martin Keown when, with only minutes left, he ballooned his close-range strike well over the bar from a matter of yards when it appeared easier to score.

And so it was to penalties. Wenger complained that the sudden-death shoot-out was deemed to be at the Gala end even though no coin toss was made. The intimidating noise may have played a part in Vieira and Suker failing to score, with only Ray Parlour successfully converting. Penbe, Şükür, Davala all scored with ease. To add insult to injury, ex-Spurs misfit Gica Popescu hit the winning spot-kick to end a miserable day and night for Arsenal FC.

Wenger said,

We had a not very good first half and in the end lost to a good Galatasaray side. We improved in the second half but really we could not find our true game today. It is very disappointing because this is the third cup we have missed this season through penalty shoot-outs. We lost in the FA Cup and the Worthington Cup in that way, too, and it is very difficult to take.

Wenger did concede, however, that the Gunners under-achieved in not managing to break through a stubborn Gala team who had Gheorghe Hagi ordered off four minutes into extra time.

'It was not a huge advantage for us to have Hagi sent off,' said Wenger. 'Sometimes you defend better with 10 men because everybody is focused. We could not take advantage because at that stage we had tired legs and could not afford to go on all-out attack for fear that we could concede a golden goal and the match would be over.'

However, the day after the game, off-field violence was back on the front pages as fighting broke out at Copenhagen Airport and bottles were thrown between fans from England and Turkey as both sets of supporters waited to board their planes. It was a sorry but all too predictable end to a depressing couple of days for the club and Arsène Wenger. When all was said and done, the club finished without a trophy for the second successive year. Yet there was some good news for Arsenal fans when the Frenchman revealed, 'When I sign a contract, it is not yes one day and no the next day. I have a contract with Arsenal until the end of the 2002 season, and I will respect it.'

Was his refusal to leave the club a tacit admission that Wenger realised new signings would have to be made to freshen the side? His ongoing passion and commitment – certainly after their defeat in a final of a tournament they hadn't envisaged competing in and off field events they wanted to forget – proved his determination to put silverware back in the trophy cabinet at Highbury.

The events of the next few seasons would reward his desire and dedication to the club.

13

Manchester United (H)

1 October 2000

Arsenal commenced their league season away to Sunderland on 18 August 2000. It was not a good day for the club. A second-half header from ex-Gunner Niall Quinn was enough to defeat Arsène Wenger's team in their first game. To make matters worse, Patrick Vieira was sent off and Wenger was involved in an altercation with fourth official Paul Taylor in the stadium tunnel. On the following Monday night, Lauren scored on his debut for Arsenal in a 2-0 win over Liverpool. But the main talking point was Vieira's second sending off in three days – which had him openly questioning his future. It was to Wenger's eternal credit that he showed great loyalty to Vieira when all and sundry outside the club were breathing fire.

Vieira showed his strength of character in his final match before his five-match suspension, scoring two goals against Charlton Athletic at Highbury in a 5-3 win.

He was coming to the end of his ban by the time Arsenal played Manchester United. Yet the way they performed on the day showed he wasn't missed. It also helped that Thierry Henry struck one of the goals of his career in a moment of genius that will be forever treasured by Gooners everywhere.

Arsenal: Seaman, Luzhny, Keown, Adams, Silvinho, Bergkamp, Grimandi, Parlour, Ljungberg, Henry, Kanu. Substitutes: Dixon, Wiltord, Vivas, Lukic, Vernazza.
Manchester United: Barthez, Irwin, G. Neville, Johnsen, Silvestre, Beckham, Scholes, Keane, Giggs, Cole, Sheringham. Substitutes: Butt, Bosnich, Yorke, Solskjaer, Brown.
Referee: Graham Barber
Attendance: 38,146

A single piece of superb skill, artistry and innovation from Arsenal's Thierry Henry won this game. It shone like a beacon amid the invariably artless physical intensity that fixtures between these two English giants often brings. It was also enough to help displace Manchester United from the top of the table, with Arsène Wenger secretly delighted that the Gunners moved level with the reigning champions on points.

Their victory at Highbury meant they had now won six successive games in all competitions at home this term.

The North Londoners owed their triumph to the traditionally labelled virtues of snatching a goal against the run of play and defend stoutly for the remainder of the game. It was the ethos that brought silverware under George Graham, yet 1-0 to Arsenal seems like a galaxy away when contrasted with the sublime football they invariably play under their French alchemist Wenger.

To claim that the Red Devils had a lot of possession would be factually correct but would not describe the whole story. The fact that United, in the second half, undeniably enjoyed territorial advantage would be to ignore the fact that they did little with it – certainly not compared to their usual high standards. Credit for this must go to the Arsenal defence, marshalled without ceremony by those two defensive workhorses Martin Keown and Tony Adams.

It was also true to say that Arsenal carved out the large number of meaningful chances during the game, and could and should have won by more than a single-goal margin.

Fabian Barthez, returning to his duty in front of the United goal after injury, showed no ill effects as he threw himself about to grand conclusion. His anticipation was excellent, as was his agility. It would have taken something special to have beaten on this form.

And it did.

Henry's finish was as sublime as it was outrageous. Yet even for someone of Henry's ability – having scored twenty-five times for his new club last term following Wenger adaption of his ex-Monaco charge to frontman from pacy but ineffective winger – the fact was Henry had not scored in his previous six games, stretching over the last month.

And for the first half hour of this passionate contest, roared on by an equally passionate crowd, Henry gave little indication that anything would change – not in the maelstrom of frenzied tackling and a lack of width.

The game threatened to proceed from niggly to downright brutish when David Beckham was yellow carded for upending Freddie Ljungberg. But Kanu played a short ball to Gilles Grimandi, who then found Henry lurking on the left-hand side of the penalty area outside the box. It was instructive to point out he had his back to goal, and no sign of danger was alerted by anyone on or off the pitch.

What happened next flowed into legend that grows on every retelling.

Henry, Arsenal's £10-million signing from Juventus, upon receiving the ball, proceeded to flick it up while simultaneously pivoting instinctively to face Barthez's goal. Before he had a chance to turn fully, his right foot came across in a sideways arc to connect perfectly with the waist-high ball.

The shot was firm but looping. Another thing in its favour was the fact that Barthez was completely unprepared for it, as he had no idea what Henry was doing until a few microseconds previously. To the utter amazement of the goalkeeper and his teammates, and to the joy and surprise of the crowd, the ball flew into the far corner of the net.

It was one of the best goals ever scored at Highbury, and definitely one of the most audacious. Highbury erupted in delight. Later even Sir Alex Ferguson tipped his hat saying, 'You can't do anything about a goal like that – I couldn't believe it.'

Wenger said after the game,

When you haven't been scoring goals, sometimes you need to try something a little bit crazy – something you don't have to think about but just do it. Thierry played with much more freedom once he had scored.

After going 1-0 down, United failed to raise their game until the second half. Yet they appeared slothful in midfield where they were usually so determined and aggressive. Even Roy Keane was not as destructive, belligerent, or most importantly, effective. Paul Scholes ferreted about but with little success.

Of course, you could argue that Beckham worked hard and that Andy Cole tried to harry Keown. But another surprise of the afternoon, bathed as it was in late autumnal sunlight, was that Arsenal fans' arch-enemy Teddy Sheringham was utterly ineffective and Ryan Giggs, ploughing a lonely furrow on the left flank, was forced to come inside in a fruitless attempt to find the ball.

Or to look at it another way, Ray Parlour and Grimandi worked so hard at denying United time and space on the ball that it fatally disrupted their natural cadences. Their efforts in subduing Keane, Scholes and Beckham were nothing short of a masterclass.

The net result was David Seaman only having to make one serious save, tipping over the bar from a Giggs shot that was always rising, having received a pinpoint cross from his fellow 'class of '92' alumni Beckham.

Once Wenger had replaced Kanu with a defender, Nelson Vivas, United found it even harder to break Arsenal down, and had Parlour not trodden on the ball after a 50-yard dash by Henry set him up for a goal, Highbury would have been spared an anxious last few minutes.

Surprisingly, given the paucity of performance from United, it was their first League defeat since February, eight months previously, when they lost 3-0 to Newcastle. They had only beaten Arsenal once in their last seven matches. 'You get these blips occasionally,' dismissed Ferguson. Yet the blips could be counted as six in seven now.

Afterwards Wenger said,

It was playing on Henry's mind he was not scoring the goals he wanted to score. And sometimes you do something completely crazy. Maybe if he'd have had a one on one with Barthez he'd have missed it. When you have a little doubt in your mind, doing something completely unexpected helps you. Just do it don't think about it. That was important for him. He's never gone through a period where he didn't score. It's the first time since he's been in this position that he didn't score for a while. It's part of the learning process. I talked to him about it. But you can say what you want – when a player is so desperate to score you can only show confidence in him. They need it to survive.

14

Valencia (A)
17 April 2001

The 2000/01 Champions League season was one of two group stages. Arsenal had successfully navigated phase one, by topping Group B ahead of Lazio, which included an impressive 2-0 home win over the Italians at Highbury, with the sparkling Swede Freddie Ljungberg netting a brace in a comprehensive evisceration of the reigning Serie A winners. Shakhtar Donetsk were beaten 3-2 in London two weeks previously in an entertaining game. Despite being 2-1 down with barely minutes remaining, Martin Keown improbably turned into a double goalscoring hero during the tie.

Arsène Wenger's men finished in first place with thirteen points and four wins, which saw them enter Group C in phase two. In a tight group dominated by Bavarian giants Bayern Munich, a crucial 1-0 away win at French Champs Lyon in February helped to clinch runners-up spot in a fraught finish to the group. With the Gunners losing 1-0 at the Olympic Stadium in Munich in their final game, Lyon failed to progress by failing to beat Spartak Moscow in the other game.

This all meant that the Londoners qualified for the Champions League, despite having the worst record of any group runner-up in the tournament's history with a measly eight points gained and a goal difference of minus two. No matter, the main thing was Arsenal now had a chance of serious progression in the continent's biggest and most prestigious tournament.

With a 2-1 over the team, they were drawn against Valencia in London with a brace from Ray Parlour, including a 30-yard piledriver past Canizares in front of the North Bank. Hopes of reaching the semi-finals were high. With Leeds United awaiting the victors, Wenger's men had never previously had a better chance of reaching a Champions League final.

Unfortunately for Arsenal, they were to meet with late heartbreak at the evocative, atmospheric Mestalla Stadium.

Valencia: Canizares, Angloma, Ayala, Pellegnno, Carboni, Angulo, Mendieta, Baraja, Vicente, Carew, Sanchez Substitutes: Djukic for Ayala, Mimar for Angulo, Zahovic for Sanchez.
Arsenal: Seaman, Dixon, Keown, Adams, Cole, Parlour, Lauren, Vieira, Pires, Wiltord, Henry. Substitutes: Ljungberg for Parlour, Kanu for Pires.
Referee: Kim Neilsen
Attendance: 47,700

Jon Brodkin's *Guardian* match report from Valencia opened,

> As the Mestalla stadium erupted in raucous, colourful celebration, the dejected look on the faces of Arsenal's players said it all. Having come within 15 minutes of their first European Cup semi-final, Arsène Wenger's team saw their dream cruelly shattered by a John Carew header that gave Valencia victory on away goals.
>
> It will scarcely dull Arsenal's pain to know that they deserved better last night and that, over the two legs, they matched Valencia goal for goal. The defiant defence and increasing confidence they displayed here were undone by the one lapse that enabled Carew to land the decisive blow and earn a semi-final tie against Leeds United.

The truth was, Arsenal had held out in valiant fashion until the tall Norwegian forward headed in Angulo's cross to break Gunners' hearts with 15 minutes left. That he nipped in ahead of Martin Keown and Tony Adams, who had defended heroically up until then, performing all manner of blocks, tackles and taking charge of organising and cajoling a resolute and disciplined rearguard, only added to the agony. However, at this level one lapse of concentration is all it takes for elimination.

It had started so well for Arsenal, with their 3,000 travelling fans mainly encamped in Manolo's bar all afternoon – the famous drummer and cheerleader for La Roja and Valencia.

In the opening stages, Valencia may have been dominant but without really carving any clear cut chances until the 25th minute, when Seaman made a superb save from Carew after a cross from Vicente.

Wenger said, 'Maybe in the first 25 minutes we were a little too deep but in the second-half we came out and played higher up the field. The crowd turned against them and we looked comfortable.'

Thierry Henry could and should have put the tie beyond the Spaniards' reach when Vieira and Wiltord worked well together to send him through, but he snatched at his shot, which ended in the side netting.

With time ticking away, and Keown and Adams in tremendous form, Arsenal started to believe a semi-final place was in their grasp. Until Carew's late intervention.

A desperately disappointed Wenger said afterwards,

> We defended well. You feel your 'keeper will have to make four or five saves at a place like this, and if you look at the number David Seaman had to make tonight it's quite surprising. But one loss of concentration cost us dearly.
>
> We didn't have the break or killer instinct to get a goal.
>
> The challenge now is to qualify again for the Champions League and to win the FA Cup.

15

Liverpool (N)

12 May 2001

Arsenal were to finish the 2000/01 season in second place on seventy points, albeit a distant ten points off Champions Manchester United. A dramatic defeat to Middlesbrough 0-3 at Highbury in April was arguably the moment the hunt for the title was conceded. Losing 1-0 to Valencia to exit the quarter-finals of the Champions League only three days later then saw the end of their European Cup ambitions. Only a win in the FA Cup final could salvage the season in terms of silverware.

The run started in Cumbria as the Gunners won 1-0 through a Sylvan Wiltord goal at blustery Brunton Park in round three. Queens Park Rangers were humiliated on home turf in the fourth round 6-0, with the away goalscorers being Pires, Bergkamp, and a brace from Wiltord. Unfortunately for the Superhoops, they were supplemented by two own goals from the Loftus Road outfit, who were anything but their nickname on the day.

Round five saw Chelsea eclipsed 3-1 in North London, with an Henry penalty and two from Wiltord, who kept up his record of scoring in every round up to then. His sequence continued when Blackburn Rovers were summarily dispatched 3-0 at Highbury in a low-key quarter-final, with a strike from the ex-Bordeaux man, Tony Adams and Pires. The run was to come to an end with a North London derby. Staged in the North West at Old Trafford, Pires and Vieira netted in a 2-1 victory to set the stage for the first FA Cup final between Arsenal and Liverpool since the late drama of the 1971 showpiece.

The year 2001 would soon join it as a memorable final – but this time it would be Liverpool fans who would recall the match with fondness.

Arsenal: Seaman, Dixon, Keown, Adams, Cole, Pires, Grimandi, Vieira, Ljungberg, Wiltord, Henry. Subtitutes: Parlour for Wiltord, Kanu for Ljungberg, Bergkamp for Dixon. Not used: Lauren, Manninger.
Liverpool: Westerveld, Babbel, Henchoz, Hyypia, Carragher, Murphy, Gerrard, Hamann, Smicer, Heskey, Owen. Subtitutes: McAllister for Hamann, Fowler for Murphy, Berger for Smicer. Not used: Arphexad, Vignal.
Attendance: 72,500

The 120th FA Cup final was the first to be staged outside England. Home for the next six years was to be the Millennium Stadium, Cardiff. An impressive stadium with a city-centre location, many fans of both sides took the opportunity to have a long weekend in the principality, enjoying the heatwave conditions and the copious restaurants, bars and clubs. It was also the first where both finalists' managers were from outside the UK.

Wenger resisted the temptation to bring back Dennis Bergkamp after a long injury absence, opting instead for the pairing of Henry and Wiltord, who had served the club well on their cup run. The Merseysiders under Gerrard Houlier chose Emile Heskey and Michael Owen up front. The decision thereby signalled his intent by calling a stop to his attacking rotation policy, leaving the Reds committed to a counter-attacking approach – ceding the North Londoners possession and space up until the final attacking third of the pitch. It was a risky strategy that threatened to backfire on Houlier in the early stages as Arsenal dominated.

Arguably, the key moment of the game came on 16 minutes, when the team from London saw a vigorous – and legitimate – penalty appeal turned down. The Swede Freddie Ljungberg sent Henry scampering clear to dance past Liverpool's Dutch goalkeeper Sander Westerveld. Henry then steadied himself before aiming his shot at the near post. To the dismay of the French forward it was stopped illegally by Swiss defender Stephane Henchoz with the inside of his left arm as he struggled to prevent himself from falling over. Henry was incredulous at the penalty not being awarded, as were many of his teammates. To add insult to injury, the referee, Gloucestershire's Steve Dunn, then awarded a goal kick. From Arsenal potentially being 1-0 up – or at the very least having a penalty awarded with the very real prospect of Henchoz being sent off – Liverpool had escaped without a scratch.

The rhythm of the game was also being stifled by the sunbaked and steamy Cardiff temperatures, which contributed to the listless and slow-moving pace of the first half, and the recently returfed pitch that sapped the legs as much as any Wembley grass ever did. The fact the pitch was effectively split in two due to the shadow running from goal-to-goal at the Millennium Stadium probably didn't help the players, spectators or the estimated five million viewers on ITV either.

Thankfully, the game sparked into life immediately after the restart as the muscular Heskey, using his undoubted strength, cleaved a way through Arsenal's defensive line only to direct a header straight at David Seaman, who pawed it to safety.

Yet it was Liverpool who were able to breathe a sigh of relief on 56 minutes, as a splendid piece of Henry magic saw him juggle the ball past Westerveld. His moment of brilliance gave ex-Junior Gunner Ashley Cole what appeared to be an easy chance. However, the footballing gods were with the Merseysiders again in Cardiff as the young left-back speared the ball towards the net – only for Liverpool captain, the Finn Sami Hypia, to prevent the ball from crossing the line by clearing his lines unceremoniously.

Hypia was again the Liverpool saviour eleven minutes later as he cleared another Arsenal effort off the line, this time with his head from a Ljungberg lob. Arsenal fans screamed their support, knowing that such intense attacking would bring its rewards. They weren't mistaken as the North Londoners finally made a deserved breakthrough with 71 minutes on the clock.

After a spell of concerted Gunners pressure, Westerveld fluffed a kick, allowing Arsenal to regain possession. A swift interchange ensued before Pires fed an advancing Ljungberg, who skilfully rounded the Dutch 'keeper before lifting his shot into the net. His run towards the delirious Arsenal fans at the end behind the goal was as much in relief as it was joy, as the big Liverpool 'keeper could only stand and shake his head in bitter disappointment at his error. Only seconds after Liverpool had kicked off again, the goalkeeper made amends by preventing a Henry shot with a point blank save. But if the Londoners thought the game was won, they were very much mistaken.

Houllier immediately made a change of personnel and tactics. By bringing on Fowler and Patrik Berger for Murphy and the ineffectual Vladimir Smicer, he belatedly decided to attack Arsenal. The adjustment was to go down in Liverpool folklore, as was a certain twenty-one-year-old Michael Owen, who capitalised on Martin Keown's misjudgement on 83 minutes when meeting a McAllister free-kick by heading into the air rather than away. The error allowed Marcus Babbel to direct the ball to Owen, who hooked a volley past a shell-shocked Seaman to make it 1-1. The momentum was now with the Merseysiders, and five minutes later, Owen scored his second. Berger played the ball from inside his half for Owen to run onto past a struggling Lee Dixon. With Tony Adams closing in but not near enough for an effective challenge, and before Seaman could gauge the angle, Owen fired the ball low into the far corner to give Liverpool an unexpected lead. In the space of five minutes, Arsenal had gone from being 1-0 up to losing 2-1.

Too stunned to attempt to restore parity, the Gunners players fell to their knees at the final whistle in disbelief. Liverpool had won the FA Cup for the sixth time in their history.

David Lacey, writing in *The Guardian,* said of Owen's two remarkable and hitherto unforeseen interventions: 'This was a comeback to rank with Blackpool in 1953 and Everton in 1966 and it is doubtful whether the Cup has ever been won with quite the panache of Owen's second goal.' Yet adding for balance, 'Had Arsenal held on to their lead no fair person could have argued that the Cup had not been won by the more positive, more imaginative side.' Gerrard Houlier simply said, 'Big players will regularly deliver in big games.'

Arsène Wenger reflected ruefully after the game: 'It was obvious that we should have won, and we had a clear penalty turned down – but this was the story of our season.' It was a season that promised so much but with the club finishing empty-handed for a third season in a row.

Thankfully for Wenger and Arsenal fans everywhere, the disappointment was to prove the stimulus for a never-to-be-forgotten campaign only months later.

16

Chelsea (N)

4 May 2002

With the title within touching distance at the end of the 2001/02 season, and a trip to Old Trafford to decide matters four days hence, Arsenal could have been forgiven for being distracted. Yet although they still needed a point from their final two games, they gave the FA Cup final their full attention at the Millennium Stadium.

With memories of their agonising first trip to Cardiff a year earlier still fresh, the Gunners were determined not to suffer the same fate twelve months on.

With Arsenal beginning their Cup run at a packed Vicarage Road, in a game that television had moved to an early kick-off in anticipation of an upset, the Londoners eased through the gears to register a 4-2 victory, with Ljungberg, Henry, Kanu and Bergkamp scoring. The fourth round saw a contentious 1-0 victory at Highbury (Bergkamp) – remembered as much for Jamie Carragher reacting to a coin being thrown onto the pitch by lobbing it back. With visitors Gillingham being crushed 5-2 in round five, with strikes from Adams, Wiltord (2), Parlour and Kanu, and a 1-1 draw at St James's Park in the sixth round, the stage was set for Robert Pires, who was arguably the most in-form player in the country, to perform his magic in the replay at Highbury. The Frenchman was rampant, netting the opener and helping with number two in the 3-0 win. However, the game was to end badly for him as he suffered a serious cruciate knee ligament injury in front of the Clock End, which would keep him out of the forthcoming Japan and Korea World Cup. Arsène Wenger was quoted after the comprehensive victory, in which Campbell and Bergkamp also scored, saying, 'I was thinking of not playing Robert in the game. I should not have.'

The Gunners, for their part, were relentless, easing past Middlesbrough in the semi-final held at Old Trafford to keep their double dreams alive as 'Boro's Gianluca Festa put through his own goal, sending the North Londoners through to their second final in two years – a feat the club had not matched since they reached three finals in a row under Terry Neil between 1978–1980.

Arsenal: Seaman, Lauren, Campbell, Adams, Cole, Wiltord, Parlour, Vieira, Ljungberg, Bergkamp, Henry. Substitutes: Edu for Bergkamp, Kanu for Henry, Keown for Wiltord. Not used: Dixon, R. Wright.
Chelsea: Cudicini, Melchiot, Gallas, Desailly, Babayaro, Gronkjaer, Lampard, Petit, Le Saux, Gudjohnsen, Hasselbaink. Substitutes: Terry for Babayaro, Zola for Hasselbaink, Zenden for Melchiot. Not used: De Goey, Jokanovic.
Attendance: 73,963

North and West London were out in force in the Welsh capital in the first all-London FA Cup final since Spurs played Queens Park Rangers in a replay at Wembley in 1982. Chelsea were to eventually finish sixth, a massive twenty-three points off Arsenal in top spot, but were determined to show to the world they could beat anyone on their day.

Chelsea, under Italian Claudio Ranieri, gambled on the fitness of Jimmy Floyd Hasselbaink, who along with Graeme Le Saux, was passed fit. A young John Terry was only able to start the game on the substitute bench after waking up that morning with a virus affecting his balance. Wenger picked first-choice goalkeeper David Seaman in place of Richard Wright, while fit-again Sol Campbell was given the nod ahead of Martin Keown at centre-half.

Le Saux, proving his injured calf was no more clattered into Lauren with a head-high challenge with only 120 seconds on the clock – rightly earning him an early booking from referee Mike Riley. Unfortunately, it was a sporadic outburst of passion in an otherwise poor first half that saw very little goalmouth action. The first 45 minutes enlivened only when Bergkamp headed over, with Blues 'keeper Carlo Cudicini stranded after Patrick Vieria's incisive pass on 21 minutes. It was followed by Sylvain Wiltord's cross on 37 minutes, which saw Lauren head over when it was easier to score.

But if the first half was inadequate for a showpiece final, the two London rivals came out fighting in the second half, both determined to win the game. Stamford Bridge custodian Cudicini showed his reflexes with a superb close-range stop from Thierry Henry moments after the second half had kicked off, as the match belatedly sprang to life.

The West Londoners were determined to put Arsenal under siege, as Icelander Eidur Gudjohnsen forced Seaman into making a high-quality save with an angled shot that narrowly failed to make it 1-0 to Chelsea. But it was clear Hasselbaink was struggling, and it was hardly surprising; Ranieri admitted his gamble had not paid-off in terms of the relying on the Dutchman's suspect fitness by replacing him for the diminutive Gianfranco Zola on 67 minutes.

Soccer AM's Tim Lovejoy, who had been commentating on the match with Arsenal fan Bradley Walsh via Sky Sports FanZone, left no one in any doubt what he thought of Ray Parlour. As Parlour, endearingly dubbed the 'Romford Pelé' by previous teammate Marc Overmars, picked up the ball outside the box with no danger apparent, Lovejoy sneered, 'it's all right, it's only Ray Parlour'. Lovejoy then proceeded to watch in disbelief as the curly haired midfielder, who never gave less than his all for the Gunners, smashed the ball into the net with a remarkable right-foot drive from 25 yards. The smug Lovejoy was speechless, possibly due to the dawning realisation he would forever be reminded of his unfounded jibe by delirious Arsenal fans.

Parlour, in an interview with the author in 2014, said of the moment,

I did send Lovejoy a poster later, which said 'It's only Ray Parlour', which was a little bit of fun – to be fair it's probably right what he said about me because if you look at the quality in our side, with the likes of Bobby Pires, Bergkamp, Henry, Vieira, people like that – they probably would have thought that they would be far more likely to score than me. It's funny but I used to score goals like that every week in training, I really did – but you always want to do it in a big game. Luckily enough it was a cracking goal – but it was an important goal too because I think at that time Chelsea were coming into it and Dave

Seaman had made a couple of important saves that kept us in it. I think the first goal was always going to win the game for either side so luckily enough it was a very important goal for us to help win the FA Cup.

Nine minutes later, Ljungberg became the first player to notch strikes in successive FA Cup finals since Bobby Smith forty years previously. Another nine minutes later, the red-haired Swede sent a sweet side-foot past Cudicini to make it 2-0, after he embarked on a surging run from the halfway line, which saw him curl the ball past Cudicini from outside the box. The popular attacking midfielder was serenaded long and loud by the estimated 25,000 Gunners fans in the ground singing:

> We love you Freddie
> 'Cos you've got red hair
> We love you Freddie
> 'Cos you're everywhere
> We love you Freddie
> 'Cos you're Arsenal through and through.

The goals deflated Chelsea, prompting many pundits to ask whether a Cup final had ever been settled by such stunning goals. As referee Riley blew the final whistle, the Arsenal fans celebrated wildly as their club claimed their eighth FA Cup win (and first part of the double) in eclipsing their London rivals. In doing so, the victory also helped banish bad memories of the previous season's last-gasp loss to Liverpool.

Arsène Wenger, interviewed afterwards said, 'We are delighted – and now we must concentrate for two more games.'

Paul Hayward wrote in the following day's *Observer*,

> Ljungberg finished on the winning side, ran as tirelessly and as imaginatively as ever, and scored a pretty neat goal into the bargain. He will probably have to change his hairstyle soon, since a red streak can no longer be a statement of individualism when half the Arsenal supporters are sporting one, but as individual performances go Ljungberg can recall this Cup final with pride.

Tim Lovejoy on the other hand, after his rude and patently incorrect summation of loyal Arsenal man Parlour, most definitely could not – as Arsenal once again proved there was only one team in London.

17

Manchester United (A)

8 May 2002

With the FA Cup final already in the bag, the North Londoners travelled to Sir Alex Ferguson's citadel, Old Trafford, four days later, with morale sky high. They required a single point to lift the title and win the third double in their history.

It was a daunting task, but the portents were favourable. Wenger's team had not lost away from home in the League that season. For the superstitious among the fans of the biggest team in London, not to mention England, they had never lost when playing in their gold away kit.

On that incredible night, despite missing defensive legend and lynchpin Tony Adams, Thierry Henry, Dennis Bergkamp and Player of the Year Robert Pires, their proud unbeaten record away from home remained intact – resulting in the League title and the double.

Arsène Wenger, speaking ahead of the game and aware as he was of the monumental significance of the match said, 'This is the season of the squad, a mental strength that has kept us together. What relaxes me is knowing the effort the team is putting in.'

Reflecting on the deliberately low-key celebrations after Cardiff he added,

The players had dinner together but everyone knew that their job was not yet done. We expect United to be at their best, don't worry about that. They won't want to lose the title on their own ground, but we don't want to lose it either. Winning the title at Old Trafford will no have special significance.

The 3,000 Gooners in the ground, the millions watching and listening around the world, the players who shared many bitter battles with United over the years, and even Wenger himself – mindful of his chief adversary Ferguson – can't have fully believed the words he uttered.

Man United: Barthez, Phil Neville, Blanc, Brown, Silvestre, Scholes, Keane, Veron, Giggs, Solskjaer, Forlan. Substitutes: van Niselrooy for Veron, Fortune for Forlan. Not used: Carroll, O'Shea, Wallwork.
Arsenal: Seaman, Lauren, Keown, Campbell, Cole, Ljungberg, Parlour, Vieira, Edu, Wiltord, Kanu. Substitute: Dixon (89) for Kanu. Not used: Jeffers, Bergkamp, Wright, Stepanovs.
Referee: Paul Durkin
Attendance: 67,580

David Lacey at Old Trafford wrote in *The Guardian*,

> One goal, another Double. Arsenal completed their winning of the FA Cup and league championship for a third time last night, and for a second under Arsène Wenger, with the added satisfaction of ending Manchester United's reign as champions in front of an Old Trafford crowd.
>
> To do so Arsenal had to first match United physically and then show that, when circumstances demanded it, they could pass the ball better. They succeeded on both counts.
>
> Historical neatness demanded Wenger's team finish the job without delay. They had won their seventh crown in 1953, Coronation year, so why not their 12th at the home of Coronation Street, and in jubilee year to boot?

Why not indeed.

Sylvain Wiltord will always be remembered with fondness in the Gunners' long and proud history after netting the goal that won the Premier League and also clinched the double at Old Trafford.

The 2001/02 title race was a nail-biting season, a roller-coaster of a ride, with the lead changing hands amid fraught tension between the two superpowers Arsenal and Manchester United. Yet in the final analysis, Arsène Wenger's Arsenal accelerated clear of both the Red Devils and Liverpool by triumphing in their last thirteen Premiership fixtures – an amazing feat.

Few outside pockets of the North West and N17 resented Arsène Wenger's attacking team and its conquests. This was because Arsenal had enlivened the Premiership with their tremendous high-tempo passing and moving style, as witnessed by them scoring in every league game – proof of their manager's extraordinary commitment to the ethos of entertaining football.

Sylvain Wiltord's goal, which came fittingly on his 100th appearance for the men from Highbury, started the title celebrations in earnest.

But before that, the Gunners had to keep their discipline and composure in the face of an early onslaught of severe physical pressure from United – Ferguson's Red Devils besmirched their reputation somewhat by acting without grace or dignity in losing their crown to the Londoners.

Afterwards, when replying to Ferguson's assertion that he possessed the best team in the League (despite Arsenal winning the title in 2002), Wenger responded with a caustic irony that still resonates: 'Everyone thinks they have the prettiest wife at home.'

In truth, it was a bitterly disappointing end to United's season that promised so much as they saw their closest rivals win the title on their own turf – and how the Arsenal fans and players loved that fact as they inflicted the Red Devils' sixth home defeat of the season.

If the first half was played out in a frenzied environment, then United were extremely fortunate to end the opening 45 minutes without a red card.

Paul Scholes, never the best tackler, was fortunate not to be red carded for a reckless assault on Edu, with Phil Neville fortuitous to be given leniency by referee Paul Durkin for a wild challenge on Sylvain Wiltord. Soon it was Roy Keane's turn to act without sense by clattering midfield powerhouse Patrick Vieira as events threatened to morph into illegality. Yet for all Manchester United's physical bluster, Wenger's tough foot soldiers were very rarely threatened in terms of conceding.

Arsenal then upped the tempo on 55 minutes, when Parlour pounced on a mistake by Silvestre. The Romford Pelé then fed Wiltord, who sent Ljungberg through by sprinting past the experienced Laurent Blanc. Fabian Barthez managed to parry Freddie's shot, but the ball fell to Wiltord, who had continued his run in the very hope the ball may spill to him, and he made no mistake by tapping the rebound into the goal.

Wiltord's historic goal launched feverish celebrations in the pubs and clubs of North London, where thousands upon thousands of Arsenal fans gathered to watch on big screens.

At Old Trafford itself, a 'Champions Section' banner was unveiled in the away end much to the undisguised glee of the travelling Gooners and, after the final whistle blew, their heroes in gold shirts raced over to celebrate one of the proudest and most stunning results in the club's history.

Arsène Wenger shook the hand of the roundly defeated Sir Alex Ferguson, then sweetly twisted the knife by speaking of the 'shift of power' from Manchester to North London.

In winning the title for a second time, Wenger said:

> I feel very happy because this team got what they deserved and we did it in style. I personally believe that what this team has achieved is tremendous and will remain in history.
>
> We have 84 points, we have played 19 games away in the league without losing one and we have scored in every game. The character of this team is extraordinary. This is not only a team of good players. It is a team of togetherness.

Despite his pre-match words he said,

> To win it at Old Trafford added a bit of style – we did it in style tonight.
>
> They never looked like threatening us. When they tried to intimidate us, we didn't react. When we scored the goal you could see they didn't have the resources to respond.

Despite a spell of desperate late pressure that amounted to not very much, Wenger's men displayed the hardiness and spirit that accompanied their undoubted finesse, flair and artistry. It was the perfect combination that won Wenger his second double in fewer than four years.

In a BBC poll that asked the question 'Who held the key to Arsenal's title triumph?' shortly after the game, Wenger topped the vote ahead of Henry, Pires and Ljungberg, so important was Wenger's presence and management deemed to be.

David Lacey's report was headlined 'Arsenal rejoice in theatre of dreams', but perhaps the most fitting headline was above Tim Rich's article in *The Independent*.

It stated truthfully, if two years too early, 'Wenger's Invincibles claim grand prize in bare knuckle title fight.'

18

Tottenham Hotpsur (H)

16 November 2002

Arsène Wenger's team had started the 2002/03 encouragingly, and after thirteen matches went into their first North London derby of the season a single point behind leaders Liverpool.

His team were an impressive seven points ahead of their main rivals in the early twenty-first century, Manchester United, who had made a stuttering start in their efforts to win the League after the Gunners had completed the double the previous term.

In the League, a 4-1 win against Leeds United in September meant the club broke the record for scoring in consecutive games (forty-seven), and away League games without defeat (twenty-two).

The North Londoners had encountered defeats, most notably against a seventeen-year-old Wayne Rooney for Everton at Goodison Park, but ahead of the fixture that meant more to fans than all others, Wenger's men were steely-eyed in their desire to wipe the floor with Spurs.

And so it proved.

Arsenal: Shaaban, Luzhny, Cygan, Campbell, Cole, Gilberto, Vieira, Ljungberg, Wiltord, Henry, Bergkamp. Substitutes: Pires for Bergkamp, Jeffers for Henry, Van Bronckhorst for Vieira. Not used: Taylor, Toure.
Tottenham: Keller, Carr, Richards, King, Bunjevcevic, Davies, Redknapp, Freund, Etherington, Sheringham, Keane. Substitutes: Poyet for Etherington, Anderton for Redknapp, Iversen for Sheringham. Not used: Perry, Hirschfeld.
Referee: Mike Riley
Attendance: 38,152

David Lacey wrote in *The Guardian,*

On Saturday Arsène Wenger's side resumed their game of leapfrog at the top of the table while Tottenham merely croaked. It may have been a North London derby but only one team was at the races once Thierry Henry had sprinted from box to box to give Arsenal an early lead with a goal born of sheer bravado.

With Sylvain Wiltord, already having a goal taken away for offside, on 13 minutes Tottenham had a throw level with Arsenal's penalty area. Vieira headed safely away and Thierry Henry picked the ball up 25 yards out – 25 yards out from the Gunners' goal line that is.

Henry immediately accelerated dribbling the ball at a fast pace, while simultaneously using his innate strength to jockey with Mathew Etherington in a white shirt in vain pursuit of the ball. Everything seemed to happen in slow motion.

The Frenchman crossed the halfway line with no one challenging him. Still no one challenged Thierry as he ran faster towards his opponent's goal, almost skipping to adjust his angle, as three defenders, including Spurs captain Stephen Carr, and England international Ledley King, in a tightly packed line assembled themselves in front of him.

Henry feinted to go right, then left, spinning the first defender and earning valuable space. Henry imperceptibly slowed before pushing the ball further to the left, an intuitive movement you cannot coach.

The Arsenal forward, who Wenger took from Juventus as a wide-man and turned into a goalscoring legend, made one last movement, which earned him a valuable fraction as the second defender's momentum took him out of a challenge. Henry, on his weaker foot no less, drilled a perfectly calibrated low shot hard past the Tottenham 'keeper's despairing right-hand dive and into the net as the stadium erupted.

Not satisfied with running half the pitch towards the North Bank, Henry turned and ran back towards the Clock End. He kept going until suddenly he found himself in front of the away fans. Henry, fed by the passionate atmosphere at grand old Highbury (the one that away fans lazily and ignorantly mocked as having no atmosphere) then slid on his knees on an impossibly cool way in raucous triumph.

It looked a like pose in honour of a goal worthy enough to commemorate with a statue. It was a pose in honour of a goal worthy enough to commemorate with a statue.

David Lacey added,

> There was not much of a pursuit when Henry, having gathered Vieira's headed clearance from Steffen Freund's throw-in, leapt out of his starting blocks near the edge of the Arsenal penalty area and just kept going. It was so much like a clip from a Road Runner cartoon that Henry should have gone 'beep-beep!'
>
> One of the best action pictures of the Arsenal team of the '30s shows Alex James streaking for goal leaving three Manchester City players, Sam Barkas, Jackie Bray and Matt Busby, looking bewildered in his wake. Goran Bunjevcevic, Ledley King and Stephen Carr were left in similar confusion as Henry kept them guessing until he had made space for a left-footed drive past Kasey Keller.
>
> As individual goals go this one might not have been in the class of Diego Maradona's outrageous dribble through the England defence in Mexico City in the 1986 World Cup, yet the moment still epitomised the qualities of speed, skill and judgment.

In such a breathless start, Spurs players lost discipline, with Simon Davies being sent off with only 27 minutes on the clock; his two yellow cards were perfectly justified.

Wenger's men were in no mood for pity as they piled forward to put their bitter rivals to the sword. The Gunners then doubled their advantage on 54 minutes, when this time Henry turned provider in squaring the ball for a rampaging Freddie Ljungberg to finish with aplomb.

Spurs were poor. Their day was encapsulated by Richards performing a terrible lob over Arsenal goalie Rami Shaaban, which was easily played away by Pascal Cygan.

Their day was to get worse on 71 minutes as the home team brutally eclipsed them with yet another polished effort as Robert Pires, Henry and Wiltord joined forces for the ex-Bordeaux man to finish emphatically from close range.

The result emphasised the chasm in North London football widening with every game played. The current double winners Arsenal were simply top class, whereas Spurs, to the embarrassment of their fans, were severely lacking in class.

A pleased Wenger said at the end of the match, 'We showed our desire is there and it was a very good performance,' adding, 'we look much more stable defensively. Henry's was a world-class goal in an outstanding team performance. Clearly we've got our confidence back.'

The moment that elevated this derby ahead of many other Arsenal victories and made it such a defining one can be found outside the Emirates today, as this comprehensive victory should be called the day a statue was born. Commemorated elegantly in bronze outside Arsenal's state-of-the-art stadium, which Arsène Wenger helped design, is the club's record goalscorer in celebratory pose in front of all those shocked Spurs fans moments after putting the Gunners in front that afternoon.

19

Inter Milan (A)

25 November 2003

This extraordinary night in the San Siro has been described by many as the best European performance in the club's history. But is easy to forget that Arsène Wenger's men would have failed to progress from the group stages had they been beaten that evening. They had fallen 0-3 at home to the Nerazzurri in the first game of the 2003/04 group stage. To simply avoid defeat in the gladiatorial arena that was the Giuseppe Meazza was going to be a tall order.

However, the Gunners had other ideas.

Shaking off injuries, Wenger's team made him and the vocal travelling fans from England proud to inflict Inter's heaviest home defeat in forty-seven years of European football.

Arsenal captain on the night, Ray Parlour led the team as Arsenal fans sang lustily: 'Five – one in the San Siro.' They also sang Thierry Henry's name long into the night, not only in the ground but in the any late night bars they could find in Milan. And so they should have done. Because Henry had proved to be the inspirational force behind this improbable rout and the undoubted star of the show. It was a thrashing so unexpected it prompted Wenger to state with a hint of incredulity in his voice afterwards: 'Not in my wildest dreams could we have predicted that sort of result.'

Inter Milan: Toldo, Cordoba, Javier Zanetti, Cannavaro, Materazzi, Brechet, Cristiano Zanetti, Lamouchi, Van der Meyde, Martins, Vieri. Substitutes: Pasquale for Cannavaro, Almeyda for Lamouchi, Cruz for Van der Meyde. Not used: Fontana, Luciano, Adani, Gonzalez.
Arsenal: Lehmann, Cole, Campbell, Toure, Cygan, Ljungberg, Parlour, Edu, Pires, Kanu, Henry. Substitutes: Silva for Kanu, Aliadiere for Henry. Not used: Stack, Keown, Clichy, Papadopulos, Hoyte.
Referee: Wolfgang Stark (Germany)
Attendance: 50,000

Henry ensured the North Londoners went ahead midway through the first half with an instinctive finish, which saw him choose his spot and side-foot the ball into the bottom corner. Inter hit back through a deflected Christian Vieri shot to make it 1-1. Unfortunately for the home team, that was to be the high point of what was to prove a miserable and humiliating night.

Arsenal went back in front on 49 minutes with a Freddie Ljungberg effort, who tapped home from yards out. For a spell, the Italians piled the pressure on to ensure some nervy moments with Lehmann alert to gathering Cannavaro's header, with Van der Meyde firing a free-kick inches over the woodwork. But the pressure was to work in Arsenal's favour as the extra space allowed them to break on the counter.

And in the 87th minute, Henry scored what was to be one of the most memorable goals in Arsenal history. Taking possession of captain Parlour's header in the middle of the pitch, the Frenchman sprinted away from his man Zanetti before halting his run. The sudden halt only served to inspire Henry while disorientating the Argentina captain, as Arsenal's maestro suddenly burst past him again to drive a left-footed shot with remarkably low backlift past 'keeper Francesco Toldo into the net via the post. The goal contained more than a few aspects of Henry's magical powers: speed, imagination, power, technique and superb finishing ability. If the night had ended there then this would still have been a memorable result and performance thanks to Henry's all-round play culminating in his solo special.

Yet Wenger's men weren't finished yet. Six minutes later, the team and fans were in wonderland as Arsenal piled forward to allow Edu to net their fourth. Two minutes later, the joy turned to disbelief as Pires slammed home, played in by substitute Jeremie Aliadiere to give the wide-man his first and his amazing team's fifth. Aliadiere was on the pitch as an 89th minute replacement for Henry as Wenger allowed a well-deserved standing ovation for the incredible Frenchman not only from Arsenal fans, but, sportingly, by the whole stadium.

The 5-1 scoreline was a perfect response to those who had questioned Wenger's teams ability in Europe. As he said afterwards, 'I am very proud of the players and the spirit they showed. Our character came out. We were persistent and we took our chances.'
And as Wenger recalled later in his Arsenal career,

> I think Alberto Zaccheroni was the Inter manager at the time and we just played them off the park. I remember we played with Edu and Ray Parlour in central midfield. Patrick Vieira didn't play.
>
> Those are the nights you don't forget – we played a fantastic game.
>
> After such a long time at a club, you think that we have basically won everywhere in Europe now. I think the only ground we haven't won at is Barcelona but we have won at Real Madrid, at Bayern Munich, at Dortmund, at Inter, at AC Milan. That was one of the big nights in Europe.

However, he added a touch ruefully,

> The players surprised some people that night, but I think that win also destabilised my team. It attracted a lot of interest from clubs and at the end of the season, we didn't have the same dressing room because all the agents started looking at our players. Sometimes, wins of that stature can be disruptive after. That can be the downside of being successful, especially when you have a young team with unexpected quality.

The captain that unforgettable night was Ray Parlour. In an interview with the author for the *Gooner* fanzine, he recalled,

> One of my proudest moments in an Arsenal shirt was when I was captain the night we went to San Siro and beat them 5-1. It was an amazing game. I always look back at that

as one of our best away performances we ever gave. They had a great side back then, an excellent side – they beat us 3-0 at Highbury earlier in the campaign so to go in their own back yard and win 5-1 – even the Italian fans at the San Siro clapped us off at the end. It was an amazing experience as a skipper of Arsenal.

He added mischievously, 'I just can't believe I didn't keep the armband! Patrick Vieira came back but I should have kept my place as skipper!'

If Parlour had kept his position as captain, nobody who witnessed Arsenal's performance that night would have complained. Certainly not the passionate fans of Inter Milan who gave Wenger and his men a richly deserved standing ovation.

20

Portsmouth (A)
6 March 2004

Arsenal were having a stellar season in the league. But it was the FA Cup sixth round at Fratton Park that proved Arsène Wenger's team were well on track for silverware that season.

The South Coast club at home was never an easy visit, with the cramped confines of a traditional English ground, fired up by a fervent but well-informed home crowd who knew good football when they saw it.

After Arsenal's crushing victory, they weren't slow in recognising they had been beaten by a far superior team performance on the day.

Portsmouth: Hislop, Pasanen, Primus, De Zeeuw, Taylor, Smertin, Faye, Quashie, Berkovic, Mornar, Yakubu. Substitutes: Stone for Berkovic, Hughes for Quashie, Sheringham for Mornar. Not used: Wapenaar, Harper.
Arsenal: Lehmann, Lauren, Campbell, Toure, Cole, Ljungberg, Vieira, Edu, Silva, Reyes, Henry. Substitutes: Bentley for Ljungberg, Clichy for Vieira, Kanu for Henry. Not used: Taylor, Cygan.
Referee: Jeff Winter
Attendance: 20,137

Kevin McCarra's post match report in *The Guardian* summed up this incredible performance:

Graceful Arsenal can make their victims feel privileged. Portsmouth are Premiership strugglers in the midst of an injury crisis and two or three other clubs might have run up this score against them, but Arsenal are alone in their capacity to make a drubbing ring out like a hymn to the marvel of football.

'The voices were in harmony. It's not a game to hate the opposition,' said Portsmouth's manager Harry Redknapp. 'It's a game we all love.'

The fraternity was recognised at this quarter-final when the Fratton Park crowd greeted the substitutions of Thierry Henry and the captain Patrick Vieira not with relief but with a standing ovation ... Detractors will snort that Portsmouth are no measure of greatness, but Wenger's men have won by the same margin against Internazionale at the San Siro this season.

The Gunners made the FA Cup semi-finals for a record twenty-fourth semi-final. It is doubtful whether many teams have ever reached the last four with such an extraordinary performance. They simply annihilated their South Coast opposition.

Portsmouth are a proud football club with loyal, passionate and knowledgeable supporters. It was to their credit that they applauded Thierry Henry and his cohort off the pitch at the end – and for that matter, during the game.

But it was a rout because Arsenal played well not because Portsmouth played badly.

Despite the greasy conditions, wide-man Jose Antonio Reyes found his feet and volleyed left-footed against the bar in the early stages. In an indication of what was to follow, Thierry Henry pounced on a deflection soon after and slotted past Shaka Hislop to make it 1-0 to Arsenal.

Pompey right-back Petri Pasanen succeeded in blocking Ljungberg's pass to Reyes with a sliding tackle. However, the ball fell benignly to Henry, who fired home with panache.

The visitors from North London, who were already playing scintillating football, carried on in the same vein, slicing through Pompey's back line virtually every time they came forward.

Ljungberg and Henry worked well in performing a polished one-two, which sent the Frenchman wider into space, allowing him to find the angle to cut the ball back for Brazilian midfielder Edu. Unfortunately for Wenger's men, Hislop did well to save the low shot. Then it was powerhouse Patrick Vieira's turn to go close, as he powered a header wide by a whisker from a corner.

The inevitable occurred for Arsène Wenger's men as they made it 2-0 on 43 minutes. Edu's trickery moved the ball between Pasanen and Linvoy Primus to Swede Freddie Ljungberg, who calmly curled the ball beyond Hislop's reach and in to the net.

'When the team plays well there is space for everyone to express himself,' said Wenger. 'Edu's vision and technique have come on very well.'

Defender Kolo Toure then struck a rare goal on half-time to emphasise the gap in class between the two teams, exploiting poor defending to make it 3-0.

The second period continued with the Gunners' clinical finishing in sharp contrast to Portsmouth's poor finishing when presented with a chance. Most significantly, when Ivica Mornar showed a lack of technique and composure in taking far too many touches, allowing the Gunners to clear their lines.

On 49 minutes, Henry made it 4-0 with his second of the afternoon, which was a masterclass in quick-thinking and anticipation. The Frenchman, faced with a clutch of defenders, simply bent a shot through the collection of opponents and past a stunned Hislop.

Ljungberg then made it 5-0 by notching his second with a deflected shot, not giving the unfortunate Hislop a chance. Wenger's men attacking threat understandably diminished slightly with the game won, allowing Pompey forward Yakubu to nod against the woodwork. Matty Taylor then struck the post with a low shot before the man Arsenal fans loved to hate, Edward Sheringham, as the late Brian Clough used to call him, came on as a substitute, and glanced the ball over Arsenal 'keeper Jens Lehmann.

The late consolation for the home team, if it was a consolation at all, failed to detract from a stunning overall performance from Wenger's side. A show that was worthy of the Pompey fans' show of appreciation.

As McCarra concluded in his *Guardian* report,

Redknapp was happy with the conclusion that they are the best team in the world at present. In the euphoria, there was a temptation to pick out a place in history for them as well and the popular comparison on Saturday was with the magnificently fluid Ajax of the early '70s.

'You don't know where you are with them,' admitted Redknapp. 'It's not as if you can squeeze up on their wide men. They've got such movement that they pop up everywhere. Henry drifts out wide and when you're attacking he's looking for space to counterattack. As soon as they get the ball, they break from everywhere.'

21

Liverpool (H)

9 April 2004

It was amazing to think that after going thirty-two games unbeaten in the 2003/04 season, Arsenal were being questioned more than ever in the title run-in.

Admittedly, they had just lost an FA Cup semi-final to Manchester United at Villa Park with an insipid display prompted by key personnel being rested, including Thierry Henry, who was benched in favour of greenhorn Jeremie Aliadiere. The reason for the decision was the huge Champions League quarter-final second-leg game against Chelsea a mere three days later.

Despite a dominant first-half performance that saw them head into the Highbury tunnel 1-0 up courtesy of a Reyes goal, Lampard netted on 50 minutes. With only 3 minutes remaining before extra time, John Terry's defensive partner Wayne Bridge netted an agonising winner for the Blues.

The 3-2 aggregate loss was compounded by the fact that supreme tinkerman, Stamford Bridge boss Claudio Ranieri, lived up to his name in the semi-final against Monaco, with some strange team choices and absurd tactics that saw the tie lost in a comprehensive 3-1 in the first leg in the principality. This could and should have been Arsenal's year in the Champions League, yet just like their defining loss to Valencia in 2001, the football gods didn't look favourably upon Wenger's team.

Yet it was still confusing. Russell Kempston wrote in *The Times,* ahead of the crucial clash with Liverpool at Highbury on Good Friday 2004,

> Can Arsenal be considered chokers? After all they did the Double only two years ago, winning the Premiership by seven points from Liverpool and beating Chelsea 2-0 in the Cup final. At the time it appeared glorious confirmation that the all-conquering rule of Manchester United was over [but] a numbing number of near misses adds weight to the theory that more often than not, Arsène Wenger's men lack what it takes when it comes to Le Crunch. They are found wanting.

Extraordinary words in a season that had seen them stretch their unbeaten League run to thirty-one games and counting.

Thankfully, they were words that were thrown back in the face of the writer after one of the most memorable games – and memorable goals – in the long and illustrious history of Highbury and Arsenal FC. A result that proved to the watching world Arsenal were back from their two previous wobbles and had no right whatsoever to be labelled chokers.

Arsenal: Lehmann, Lauren, Campbell, Toure, Cole, Ljungberg, Vieira, Silva, Pires, Bergkamp, Henry. Substitutes: Edu for Pires, Keown for Ljungberg. Not used: Reyes, Clichy, Shaaban.

Liverpool: Dudek, Carragher, Hyypia, Biscan, Riise, Diouf, Hamann, Gerrard, Kewell, Heskey, Owen. Substitutes: Baros for Heskey, Murphy for Diouf. Not used: Henchoz, Cheyrou, Luzi Bernardi.

Referee: Alan Wiley

Attendance: 38,119

Doom-monger-in-chief Mr Kempston's match report in *The Times* the day after such a momentous game read:

> After Shocking Saturday and Terrible Tuesday it was a Good Friday for Arsenal. It could have been Forlorn Friday, when they ventured another sickly step towards to the abyss, when a third defeat in seven days could have too much to take, but the good ship Arsenal righted itself and all is now well in London N5.
>
> A hat-trick from Thierry Henry, provided the highlight of a 4-2 victory against Liverpool at Highbury that not only re-established Arsenal's title credentials but also cocked a snook at the critics who predicated their recent loss of form could be permanent rather than a temporary blip... the ruthless manner in which Arsenal finally dispatched Liverpool after a tepid first half that produced a 2-1 deficit and had the doubters gleefully doubting again, left little room for argument.

It was no surprise that the rapidly growing legend of Thierry Henry added another chapter to this game. Hauling his club back into the game, which they had seemed on the verging of throwing away in the most incredible fashion, also helped provide his team with a galvanising victory; the effects on morale were almost as important as the three points themselves.

The triumph opened up a seven-point lead that had Wenger drooling afterwards:

> Thierry was brilliant. He can be a victim of his own success because if he is not scoring all the time, people ask questions.
>
> This was his most vital game of the season.
>
> It was a massive test when we went 2-1 down.

Indeed it was. Mr Kempston concluded, 'A season that was stripped almost bare on Saturday and Tuesday was revitalised yesterday.'

Thanks to Thierry Henry's dramatic – and world-class – intervention it certainly was.

Liverpool started quickest, scoring after only five minutes through Sami Hyypia. After three corners in quick succession, Steven Gerrard fed the big Finn from Harry Kewell, who notched emphatically with a diving header.

Wenger's men were stunned. A clever piece of Sol Campbell defending prevented the diminutive Michael Owen from making it two after John Arne Riise played a through ball that sliced open the Gunners' defence.

Jens Lehmann was lucky to see an Owen shot loop over after an uncertain intervention from the German.

However, on 31 minutes, Brazilian Gilberto stole the ball from Dietmar Hamann, and as Roberto Pires picked the ball up to provide Henry with a chance, he slotted past Dudek easily. The relief was tangible, but it didn't stop Arsenal from conceding a second on 42 minutes, when Owen ran through to score Liverpool's second.

Half-time came not a minute too soon for Arsenal. This was the defining moment of their season – a season where they had remained unbeaten so far, but they needed to respond now. Whatever Wenger said to them at half-time prompted a magnificent response that would be talked about for years to come; they swept Liverpool away with a majestic second-half performance, one of the best performances by an Arsenal side – ever.

What character they showed when many critics doubted them. What bravery to respond to such a perilous position by continuing to play expansive, attacking football, whose virtues were constantly espoused by their leader Wenger.

Firstly, Henry and Ljungberg joined forces on 49 minutes in allowing Pires to finish with aplomb to pull the score back to 2-2. With the crowd still celebrating, sixty seconds later came one of the best goals in the club's history – and one of the most important, too.

Henry decided enough was enough and scored one of Highbury's greatest goals. Beating five Liverpool players, including Jamie Carragher (twice), he slotted the ball past Dudek after a mazy, heart-stopping, life-affirming run that had the crowd roaring as loud a celebration as anyone had heard at the venerable old ground.

Henry then completed his treble to clinch a vital victory, capitalising on sloppy marking after Dennis Bergkamp's through ball to fire into the net on 78 minutes to make it 4-2.

No one present would ever forget Henry's second goal or the match itself, won by Wenger's men simply because they were more determined to do so.

A clearly relieved Wenger said afterwards,

I felt the way they responded was absolutely magnificent.

The togetherness of this side is unbelievable. I'm a great admirer of their human qualities and what show with their backs-to-the-wall.

When you suffer disappointments you look at how players react and their team spirit.

While Liverpool manager Gerrard Houlier said honestly, and with a touch of class, to Liverpool's *Daily Post*,

I thought Arsenal were simply stunning in the second half. It was the best I have ever seen against my team. They reacted like a wounded animal. I don't think any team could have competed with Arsenal in that form – we knew they were good but that was everything I feared from them after their two disappointments.

Today we've got to praise Arsenal.

Based on their second-half performance and Henry's stunning goals, Arsenal deserved such high praise from such a rival.

22

Leeds United (H)
16 April 2004

A hard-fought 0-0 draw on Easter Monday in the North East at St James's Park kept Arsène Wenger's men unbeaten in the League, but it was imperative that Arsenal won their next game. If results worked out, there was a chance that the League title could be won the week after at the home of their deadliest local rivals: Tottenham Hotspur. It was a thought too delicious to contemplate before the Leeds game. The game was to be played on a Friday night, which contributed to the raucous atmosphere inside Highbury, but the only thing that mattered that night was for the Gunners to gain three points to move a step closer to being Champions again.

It was a night that turned into a Thierry Henry masterclass.

Arsenal: Lehmann, Clichy, Campbell, Pires, Vieira, Toure, Gilberto, Lauren, Bergkamp, Henry, Wiltord. Substitutes: Parlour for Pires, Reyes for Bergkamp, Edu for Gilberto. Not used: Stack, Keown.
Leeds United: Robinson, Matteo, Caldwell, Kelly, Radebe, Harte, Duberry, Pennant, Milner, Smith, Viduka. Substitutes: Johnson for Viduka, Barmby for Radebe. Not used: Carson, Kilgallon, Lennon.
Referee: Dermot Gallagher
Attendance: 38,094

John Brodkin wrote in his match report for *The Guardian,*

When Arsenal lifted the championship trophy in 2002, the players bowed to the injured Robert Pires in recognition of the part he played in that success. This time they will surely fall at the feet of Thierry Henry. For all that this season has been a team effort at Highbury, the France striker stands out. By scoring four goals last night he moved Arsenal even closer to the title and left Leeds's Premiership place looking more vulnerable than ever.

Not content with completing his second hat-trick in three matches, Henry went one better this time to take his season's tally to thirty-eight, two fewer than Leeds have managed as a whole team. When questions were asked of Arsenal before and during their most recent game at home to Liverpool, it was Henry who responded with a brilliant treble. Here again he was the star, and, as against Liverpool, the impressive Pires scored the other goal.

Arsenal were utterly dominant in the game against a poor and dispirited Leeds United side that did nothing to aid their cause of avoiding relegation and a financial abyss that was looming due to what their previous chairman, Peter Risdale, described as 'chasing the dream'. With Arsenal's finances as tight as ever, and money being channelled towards the new stadium, it is worth remembering the incredible job Wenger did at this time in terms balancing budgets, but also building a team for a relative pittance that played such coruscating – and successful – football.

The Gunners were simply breathtaking as they dismissed the visitors with panache and vigour. In the opening exchanges, Arsenal signalled their intent as Clichy chased down Gary Kelly attempting to clear his lines, resulting in the ball falling for Pires who crossed for Wiltord. Despite glancing the ball goalwards, there was no one to tap it into the net.

But the miss only delayed the inevitable as Robert Pires opened the floodgates on only six minutes, following a superb through ball from the Gunners' Dutch master Dennis Bergkamp. The French wide-man took the ball cleanly before opening his body up to curl the ball beyond Paul Robinson in the United goal. His eighteenth strike of the season was a thing of rare beauty – yet the Gunners had only just started their night's work.

Wenger's side may have gone into the match with an advantageous seven-point lead but goals were the only thing on their minds once they went 1-0 up, banishing any jitters in the process.

In the 27th minute, Arsenal's Brazilian defensive midfielder Gilberto fed Henry as he latched onto the pass by accelerating beyond the single-paced Leeds defence. He slotted past an increasingly beleaguered Robinson to make it 2-0.

The strike took him to 150 goals in only 251 appearances for the club he joined as a dispirited young winger in the summer of 1999 – Wenger pulled a tactical masterstroke by moving the flying Frenchman inside, bolstering his confidence through his utter belief in Henry's ability. Henry may have far exceeded expectations, but Wenger deserves massive amounts of credit for being such a bold orchestrator. It was a move that not only brought considerable joy and silverware to the club but arguably changed the course of the Gunners' history during that time.

Henry soon chased down his thirty-sixth goal of a brilliant season. With 12 minutes to go until half-time, Bergkamp, who was also having an excellent game, playing between the lines off the main strikers in a role he revelled, played a one-two with Wiltord just outside the box before lifting the ball into the area only for a ponderous Duberry to handle.

Henry scored the resultant penalty, awarded by Dermot Gallagher, with the cheekiest of chips straight down the middle with a Panenka-style dink to make it 3-0. There was then time for Vieira to thud a header against the woodwork before the interval brought respite for an increasingly shell-shocked Leeds.

Five minutes after the break, the Frenchman achieved his hat-trick as Wiltord nudged a ball to a rampant Henry, who showed exceptional acceleration, running past static United defenders before exuberantly stretching to finish by firing the ball under Robinson's frame.

It was the first time a Gunners player had scored back-to-back Highbury hat-tricks since Doug Lishman in November 1951, when he struck trebles against West Brom in a 6-3 win and Bolton Wanderers in a 4-2 triumph. Henry's first treble was achieved in the maelstrom of a potentially faltering title chase against their main rival, with his second gained against what could have been an obdurate relegation-threatened side. As it was, Leeds United raised the white flag as they seemed to realise they were bound for oblivion both on and off the pitch.

However, the marvellous Henry was still not finished. As the joyous Highbury crowd contemplated continuing the celebrations well into a North London Friday night, he made it four for himself and five on the evening.

Robert Pires pushed the ball into his path in midfield, as Henry again used his tremendous powers of acceleration to race past a tiring and stricken Kelly. As Kelly went to trip him, Henry used all his strength and balance to stay on his feet for a fraction of a second longer to drive the ball past an onrushing Robinson. His fourth signalled another record: the first Gunner to hit a quadruple since Ian Wright achieved the feat against Everton in December 1991.

As Gallagher blew the whistle to put Leeds out of their misery, many in the ground knew they were watching the best football Arsenal had played for many a year.

As a clearly impressed Wenger said afterwards,

It's difficult to find each time new words for Thierry. Rather than talking about him, it's better watching him. When the team is on the same wavelength, with his power and pace and skills, it's a joy to watch. We have many players who can put him through.

   His finishing gets better and I think in recent games he's come back to a more central position again. For a while he went systematically out wide left. With a more central position he's more dangerous.

This side under Wenger was heading for immortality and a chance to win the League at White Hart Lane for the second time in the club's history the following week.

23

Tottenham Hotspur (A)

25 April 2004

With Newcastle United beating Chelsea ahead of kick-off, it meant Arsenal would start the match nine points ahead of the Blues. It also ensured that Arsène Wenger's side required a single point to capture the League title for the thirteenth time.

The fact they could do this at the home of their bitter North London rivals – for potentially the second time, after achieving the same feat during the club's march to the double in 1971 – only heightened the sense of expectation, and tension, in N17.

The momentous 90 minutes that followed would prove a memorable and defining afternoon for the club on the day they became Champions of England – a day that would be remembered for as long as Arsenal FC existed, as the best team in England proved beyond all doubt that North London was most definitely red.

Tottenham Hotspur: Keller, Kelly, Gardner, King, Taricco, Davies, Redknapp, Brown, Jackson, Keane, Kanoute. Substitutes: Defoe for Jackson, Poyet for Kelly, Bunjevevic for Taricco. Not used: Hirschfield, Ricketts.
Arsenal: Lehmann, Lauren, Toure, Campbell, Cole, Parlour, Vieira, Gilberto, Pires, Bergkamp, Henry. Substitutes: Edu for Parlour, Reyes for Henry. Not used: Stack, Keown, Clichy.
Referee: Mark Halsey
Attendance: 36,097

With Newcastle's result filtering through just before kick-off, Arsenal were determined to do all they could to win the title at White Hart Lane.

The opening exchanges confirmed they were deadly serious in their pursuit of their ambitions. With less than 180 seconds gone, Thierry Henry collected the ball just outside his own box, before commencing an all-encompassing passage of play that culminated in Vieira scoring past Keller via a Bergkamp cross. Just to prove the sweeping nature of the move, from Henry gathering the ball to Vieira scoring, was timed at an incredible eleven seconds.

The scoreline of 1-0 to Arsenal became 2-0 with ten minutes still to play before half-time. Bergkamp, again revelling in his role as tormentor in chief of Spurs, fed Vieira charge through the Spurs' defensive lines as if they were invisible. He then played the ball back to Pires, who had ghosted into the box to allow him to side-foot home.

At 2-0 up, with the title in sight, the 3,000 Gooners in the ground, including myself, started taunting the home fans by reminding them vociferously that it was forty-three years and counting since they last won in the League.

It was understandable, with the title seemingly won, that Arsenal's intensity dropped slightly, allowing Jamie Redknapp to fire home on 62 minutes with a low drive from outside the area, which Lehmann, who was having one of his more truculent and fractious games, perhaps should have done better to stop.

It was also understandable that Spurs would then target him in their attempt to level the scores. This is exactly what occurred in the 90th minute when Keane, unobserved by any of the officials, raked his studs down Lehmann's leg while engaged in an unseemly jostling match awaiting an injury time corner. After booking both Keane and Lehmann, referee Mark Halsey had no option but to point to the penalty spot. Keane then netted to ensure the final score would be 2-2.

But what was not understandable was the Lilywhites' over-the-top celebrations, which prompted more than one writer present to note with a frown: 'From White Hart Lane's celebrations you would have thought Tottenham had just secured the title themselves', *The Times'* Matt Dickinson noted with a Sahara-dry wit.

What was also incredible was the Argentine defender Taricco, who prior to the equaliser had suffered a torrid chasing from the Arsenal forward line, but was now indelibly involved in his team's celebrations, actually managed to pull his hamstring in his fervent merriment.

A clearly incensed Henry, to his eternal credit – despite being warned by the authorities beforehand – gathered his troops together at the final whistle and took them to the now celebrating corner where the Arsenal fans were congregated. Henry, showing leadership skills that proved you didn't have to be captain to be a leader of men, then told his men to celebrate long and hard on the White Hart Lane turf.

As he said afterwards, in a thinly veiled nod at Tarico's ridiculous behaviour, 'When you see behaviour like that it is impossible for us not to celebrate in response.'

Ray Parlour, in an interview with the author for the *Gooner* concurred,

> We just thought how can you not celebrate winning the league at White Hart Lane? We certainly made sure we celebrated after. I knew how big the rivalry was between the two teams growing up as a young Arsenal player, and we knew how special a triumph like that was for the fans as well – so we certainly made sure we enjoyed winning the league at White Hart Lane!

As the final whistle was blown, indicating Arsenal had become Champions of England at White Hart Lane, Arsène Wenger, the arch perfectionist that he is, actually slapped his thigh in frustration of Lehmann's actions, which denied a win.

There are no records of how many times a manager of a title-winning side has carried out such an action immediately after winning the League, but it provided a tremendous insight as to how much of an obsessive purist Wenger was and is.

As he said afterwards, 'That tarnished it a bit at first. It has become a game to wind him up.' Yet it did not take long for such a minor quibble to give way to the hugely fulfilling realisation that his team were now Champions.

He said with feeling, 'I don't want to diminish my other two championships but this is special.'

Tottenham fans, mirroring their team's embarrassing over-the-top celebrations at achieving a draw against the Champions at the final whistle, claimed that they had restored a semblance of pride.

It was utter and arrant nonsense. Arsenal had won the league at White Hart Lane for the second time in the history of the North London derby – that was all that ultimately mattered. And it was Arsenal celebrations at the end of game that proved that emphatic fact.

For the thirteenth time in the club's extensive and distinguished history, Arsenal FC were Champions of England.

Wenger said,

> The overall achievement of the club has been tremendous. The championship is where you see how good a team is. All the players have had a remarkable attitude and all my staff have been fantastic.
>
> We've been remarkably consistent, haven't lost a game and we have played stylish football. We have entertained people who just love football.

Wenger himself joined in the vigorous revelries with the players afterwards, and in a shot that encapsulated that era at Arsenal was photographed with his hands in the air in triumph in front of the celebrating Gooners. In the background is a flag raised proudly by the fans.

It read simply: 'Arsène Knows.'

When asked whether his team would be celebrating the title that night, a deadly serious Wenger added, 'No champagne just water.'

It was uncertain whether one of his stalwarts heeded his advice. In an interview with author for the *Gooner* years later, Ray Parlour when questioned as to how he celebrated that night recalled with a smile, 'What did I do that night? I don't know! I think I went out and celebrated for about three days afterwards!'

Despite well-deserved celebrations, Parlour and his teammates knew their manager's goal was now to achieve what was previously thought impossible: to remain unbeaten throughout a thirty-eight-match League campaign – an accomplishment that would turn an extraordinary season into an immortal one. One that would see them labelled for all eternity as The Invincibles.

24

Leicester City (H)

15 May 2004

After the title was clinched on that decisive afternoon at White Hart Lane, Arsène Wenger's men had to avoid defeat in their remaining four matches for them to end the League season unbeaten. In October 2002, Wenger had the honesty to say to the press that remaining unbeaten throughout a League campaign was possible. He was roundly derided and condemned for his words, which were seen as arrogance. Yet they were anything but.

Wenger, who always spoke truthfully to the press on any matter raised, from world politics to economics to non-League football, was criticised for articulating his firmly held belief that he had a special squad that had the potential to avoid losing over the course of a League season. There is a huge difference between hubris and quiet confidence – a fact that many who should have known better chose to ignore.

Fast forward eighteen months. Incredibly, with thirty-seven matches played and no defeats, a win or draw against Leicester City would see those words come true. As Wenger said in the aftermath of winning the title at White Hart Lane,

> The overall achievement of the club has been tremendous. The championship is where you see how good a team is. All the players have had a remarkable attitude and all my staff have been fantastic. We've been remarkably consistent, haven't lost a game and we have played stylish football. We have entertained people who just love football.
>
> I believe we must keep our humility and wonder how we can become a better team. That starts with me – if we do that then I believe there is a lot more to come from this side.
>
> My target now is to keep the players focused on our unbeaten record. We have put so much effort into this season so to lose a game now because we had switched off would not be ideal. We have to keep going.

As for anyone who has worked long and hard to reach a long-held target, ambition or goal, whether it be in a career, sport or life in general, the hardest thing can be trying to raise yourselves for more mundane ventures once a long-standing goal has been met and the initial rush of adrenaline long dissipated. The Gunners weren't immune to that familiar affliction.

They struggled in a flat 0-0 against Birmingham City at Highbury. For the insipid deadlock against Steve Bruce's side a week after White Hart Lane, to come anywhere near to that scoreless nadir showed how draining it was to lift the title.

Yet the Gunners of the 2003/04 vintage were as mentally tough as they were skilful.

Emerging unbeaten from tricky trips to Portsmouth on a foul night on the South Coast, where an early Reyes goal kept the run going for a 1-0 win at Loftus Road, against a

Fulham team having their spiritual home of Craven Cottage renovated, saw Arsenal fans in party mood – and fancy dress.

As the final whistle blew in West London, home fans saw the strange sight of inebriated pink panthers hugging bearded nuns, and deranged matadors cuddling rotund skeletons and unconvincing Mexicans. It was that type of day – it was that type of season.

But, as Leicester approached, the tone turned deadly serious once more – for a victory (or draw) would see Wenger's team become, in his words, 'immortal'.

Arsenal: Lehmann, Lauren, Toure, Campbell, Cole, Ljungberg, Silva, Vieira, Pires, Bergkamp, Henry. Substitutes: Edu for Pires, Reyes for Bergkamp, Keown for Ljungberg. Not used: Parlour, Stack.
Leicester City: Walker, Sinclair, Heath, Dabizas, Stewart, Scowcroft, Freund, McKinlay, Nalis, Bent, Dickov. Substitutes: Brooker for Freund, Coyne for Walker, Benjamin for Dickov. Not used: Gillespie, Guppy.
Referee: Paul Durkin
Attendance: 38,419

Amy Lawrence spoke for all Arsenal fans in her *Observer* piece the next morning:

While his immortals can-canned in the sun, Arsène Wenger stood awkwardly in front of his dugout and didn't know where to look. The mastermind behind one of the most remarkable feats in English football couldn't take it in at all. 'I was shocked,' he said. 'My dream was always to go through a whole season unbeaten. It's beyond belief. Not many managers can say they did that.'

Not once in 38 games of high tempo, highly charged Premiership football did Arsenal lose their nerve, their quality, and most astonishingly of all they didn't even have a moment when they were crushed by a bad bounce or a bad decision throughout nine months of competition. 'We are unbeatable,' chorused the North Bank to the Clock End as the Premiership trophy was carried on to the turf.

Some 1,060,444 fortunate souls who have clicked through the Highbury turnstiles will not easily forget the procession that was 2003/04. Nor will a squad of players who were written off nine months ago as broken, bruised, bottlers.

An expectant Highbury, in full party mode, serenaded the League winners with a resounding chorus of a song that all Gooners know off by heart: 'We won the League/At White Hart Lane...' But would they win the League by going unbeaten all season? At 1-0 down at half-time, it was debatable.

Ex-Gunner, the diminutive but tough Paul Dickov tried to put a huge dent in the club's title celebrations by netting with a header from a Frank Sinclair cross. During half-time strong words were spoken in the confines of the inner sanctum as the players and Wenger decided now was not the time to throw away 3,500 minutes of unbeaten League football. 'A revolt,' was how the Frenchman described the intense atmosphere during the break.
On this gloriously sunny day, their half-time passion proved Arsenal were determined not to be denied. Two minutes after the restart, Thierry Henry netted from the sport for his thirty-ninth goal of a record breaking season after Sinclair had brought down Arsenal's left back. From that

moment on, the unbeaten record was on its way to Highbury. Bergkamp's vision spotted Vieira embarking on a powering run, and the Dutchman fed his with an exquisitely timed through ball. The French midfield general, showing he was more than just an enforcer – a fact that every Arsenal fan knew anyway – took the ball in his stride and glanced it over an onrushing Walker to put the Gunners 2-1 up. As the fans celebrated with a thunderous round of 'Champions' and 'We are unbeatable' – the repetition of both increasing in intensity with every new rendition – the final few minutes were as joyous as celebration a anyone could remember.

A massive 250,000 fans attended the victory parade the next morning in Upper Street – some no doubt with the mother of all hangovers – the procession culminating with the trophies being displayed to the enormous crowds around Islington Town Hall. 'Now I know why we need a bigger stadium,' joked Wenger to deafening acclaim.

Yet the festivities against Leicester as the match drew to an end were enlivened further when an old George Graham player came on. Martin Keown had left the club as a callow and headstrong teenager over a difference of £50 a week in wages, but had returned to give such service to the club, to Graham and to Arsène Wenger. He came on as substitute for his tenth appearance of the season – thereby qualifying for a title winners' medal. There was a spot of comic relief as the playful Ray Parlour, who was also on the subs bench that afternoon, pretended Wenger had told him to go and started stripping off his tracksuit in preparation for an appearance. As the Romford Pelé recounted after the game, 'Martin went mental as he thought he wouldn't get his medal – you should have seen his face when he realised I was joking!'

As Wenger said afterwards, 'To improve on this in the Championship is nearly impossible, but we can win new trophies. I still have problems to realise what we have achieved. I can only say how proud I am of my players.'

Sol Campbell, in an interview with the author years later, still decried the fact that this side did not receive the praise it was due. He told me incredulously, 'To finish up not getting beaten – it was a remarkable achievement. I know people don't realise now what an achievement that was – but I think in twenty to thirty years' time people will look back and say what an achievement it really was. I was privileged to be part of that team. Happy to be in history. Happy to be among it. You just think: "Wow this doesn't happen every day." And to be there and be a big part of it was brilliant.'

As Wenger added afterwards,

> There was scepticism when I arrived in England but this is the biggest moment since I arrived here. My dream has always been to play a whole season unbeaten. It's something unique, because no other manager can say that in the top league. I'm very, very happy. I'm proud of my players.

Wenger and Arsenal had become the first side to go through a League season undefeated since Preston North End achieved the feat in 1888/89. History had been made. The litany of results read: Played 38, Won 26, Drew 12, Lost 0.

The team of 2003/04 that represented Arsenal FC that unforgettable season with such panache, such mental strength and such tenacity and will to win, allied with pure technique, skill, courage and application – had become immortal.

In becoming invincible they had become 'The Invincibles'.

25

Middlesbrough (H)

22 August 2004

The first game of the season at Highbury saw a raft of awards given to Arsène Wenger's Invincibles – past and present.

The last time an Arsenal played a League game at the stadium, it culminated in Patrick Vieira lifting the Premiership trophy above his head to an adoring public. The 2004/05 season continued in the same vein prior to kick-off. Firstly, German 'keeper Jens Lehmann was given the Golden Glove award as the custodian with the most clean sheets in the Premiership the previous term.

Then, predictably given the season he had, Thierry Henry was handed the Golden Shoe, the prize bestowed on the player who finished as European football's top scorer. Henry was also conferred Arsenal's Player of the Season award for the historic 2003/04 season.

Patrick Vieira then got in on the act, being presented with a smaller replica of the Premiership trophy to mark the current Champions' unbeaten year.

The cheers didn't end there either as Ray Parlour, the Romford Pelé so fondly christened by his teammate Marc Overmars with the moniker used by everyone, was back at Highbury after his summer move to Middlesbrough, who he would lead to a UEFA Cup final that year. The true Arsenal man looked visibly moved by his warm ovation from the crowd, who recognise loyal service to the cause more than most sets of fans.

If the Gunners succeeded in finishing the game unbeaten they would equal the all-time record of Brian Clough's Nottingham Forest team of the late seventies, which stretched to an incredible forty-two matches.

At the end of a remarkable but draining 90 minutes in the summer heat, the Gunners achieved the record. But not without being tested to their very limits by an audacious 'Boro side who would prove their pedigree that season in Europe.

Arsenal: Lehmann, Cole, Cygan, Toure, Lauren, Ljungberg, Fabregas Soler, Silva, Reyes, Bergkamp, Henry. Substitutes: Pires for Ljungberg, Flamini for Reyes. Not used: Van Persie, Almunia, Hoyte.
Middlesbrough: Schwarzer, Queudrue, Cooper, Riggott, Reiziger, Boateng, Parlour, Mendieta, Zenden, Hasselbaink, Job. Substitutes: Parnaby for Reiziger, Nemeth for Zenden. Not used: Maccarone, Nash, Doriva.
Referee: Steve Dunn
Attendance: 37,415

Kevin McCarra wrote in *The Guardian*,

It was not enough for Arsenal to make their mark by pulling level with Nottingham Forest's record of 42 League matches undefeated. They also had to sear the memory of this game itself into the mind. Splendour will always count for more than statistics.

It will be left to pedants to mutter about the champions' defending. Everyone else who spilled out into North London was babbling over the sheer spectacle. Beforehand Arsenal had received a cheque to reward their disciplinary record and a trophy to mark the unbeaten passage to last season's title, but they needed no help to foster a sense of occasion … we are watching a team unleashed.

'Unleashed' was certainly the appropriate word as the Gunners came flying out of the traps in their first game of the season, smashing Everton 4-1 at Goodison Park. Therefore it was to be no shock when Wenger kept faith with the same team that started the season so fluently in Merseyside.

Patrick Vieira was missing due to a groin injury, while Edu was not considered after playing for Brazil in Haiti on the Wednesday prior this televised Sunday game. The upshot was a third start on the trot for Cesc Fabregas. Unfortunately, the same did not apply for his stupendous mullet, which met a sad but all too predictable demise ahead of the game.

The Arsenal website defined this memorable game as 'One-nil up and cruising. Three-one down and crumbling. And, finally, a rousing comeback from an Arsenal team which proved once again that is possesses character as well as class.' It was a succinct summation of the drama in as action packed a match as any during Wenger's long reign.

It was a drama that started when Thierry Henry gave Arsenal the lead on 25 minutes; he chipped 'Boro's Australian 'keeper Mark Schwarzer after an angular raking pass from Reyes. That was no mean feat, considering the Sydney-born stopper was nearly 6 foot 5 inches – nor the fact that Henry calmly let the ball bounce ahead of an onrushing Schwarzer.

However, in a clue as to how the afternoon would unfold, the travellers from industrial Teeside manufactured an equaliser through Joseph-Désiré Job's powerful drive past Jens Lehmann from an acute angle – completely against the run of play.

Moments before half-time, Henry nearly made it 2-1 as he fired a free-kick over the 'Boro wall – the 'keeper was beaten but the ball struck the woodwork before bouncing away.

Job's strike galvanised 'Boro, and five minutes in the second period, they took an unexpected lead. Frenchman Franck Queudrue was involved, mirroring Reyes' diagonal through pass in Henry's opening goal, to find Jimmy Floyd Hasselbaink. With Pascal Cygan and Ashley Cole involved in unconvincing defensive work, Hasselbaink then drove on towards Lehmann before firing an unstoppable strike past the 'keeper.

A mere 180 seconds later, Highbury was stunned as Steve McClaren's men went 3-1 up. This time Queudrue was provider turned goalscorer as he perceptively noted Lehmann inching away from his line as he anticipated a cross, only for 'Boro's Frenchman to strike the ball with the outside of his left-foot towards Lehman's goal. With the German incorrectly positioned and wrong-footed, and the ball curving away from him, Queudrue could celebrate an ingenious goal that saw the ball nestle in the bottom right-hand corner of the net.

Arsenal appeared to be wobbling, but the majority of Wenger's men weren't known as the Invincibles for nothing. Summoning up spirit, desire, motivation and power, they regrouped to provide an amazing finale for the worried Highbury crowd, jelped by 'Boro's hitherto steadfast defence crumbling under such intense pressure and passionate crowd support.

Bergkamp made it 2-3 by shooting into the corner, after being ceded far too much space on the edge of the box by a tiring 'Boro defence, who visibly wilted in the heat and the Gunners' onslaught.

Then Pires tapped home to level the scores 3-3 after tidy work by Henry. Reyes then sent the crowd wild with relief as he edged Arsenal ahead with an impressive rising drive, made all the sweeter by having been struck with his weaker foot.

Who else but Henry made it 5-3 as he touched the ball home.

Highbury was relieved. Highbury was happy. Arsenal under Wenger had made more history. It was a result that was tough on 'Boro but showed why Arsenal were set to surpass Forest's stunning record lasting twenty-five years.

26

Tottenham Hotpsur (A)

13 November 2004

This North London derby took place only two League games after their tempestuous 2-0 loss at Old Trafford, which halted the Gunners' forty-nine-match unbeaten run. The team had drawn both a 2-2 deadlock at Highbury against Southampton and a dire 1-1 stalemate at Selhurst Park. Rather like erratic behaviour following the onset of delayed shock, this game saw an outburst of goals that no one saw coming – certainly not with the contest only registering a single goal up to the 44th minute.

Not that any Arsenal fan was complaining. After all, a win at White Hart Lane is not something be scoffed at. However, the aggregate of goals that came in this game will ensure it goes down in history as one of the most entertaining derbies in the long sequence of the fixture. It was a game that took place only seven months short months after Arsène Wenger's Invincibles took the title on the home of their bitter rivals.

That Wenger's 2004/05 vintage edged this nine-goal thriller was far more to do with their attacking flair than their customary defensive nous, which went missing for this early kick-off on a crisp autumnal day in N17.

The victory sent them top, albeit on a short-lived basis. There was even a modicum of relief their Old Trafford loss hadn't cost them any apparent offensive fluidity.

Wenger recalled his familiar line-up, despite his youngsters winning the 3-1 Carling Cup over Everton only four days previously. Robert Pires started the North London derby on the bench, with his place on the left side of midfield taken by Jose Antonio Reyes, with Dennis Bergkamp partnering Henry up front.

Tottenham Hotspur: Robinson, Pamarot, Naybet, King, Edman, Pedro Mendes, Brown, Carrick, Ziegler, Keane, Defoe. Substitutes: Davies for Pedro Mendes, Kanoute for Brown, Gardner for Keane. Not used: Redknapp, Fulop.
Arsenal: Lehmann, Lauren, Toure, Cygan, Cole, Ljungberg, Vieira, Fabregas, Reyes, Bergkamp, Henry. Substitutes: Pires for Reyes, Van Persie for Bergkamp. Not used: Flamini, Almunia, Hoyte.
Referee: Steve Bennett
Attendance: 36,095

Kevin McCarra had written in his *Guardian* match report,

It as well that there were enough goals to make Spurs fans woozy. Those people left the ground gratefully unable to focus on the fact that Arsenal had just won there for the first time since May 1999. Since this was a match like hardly any other, it even felt pedantic to count it as a fifth consecutive Premiership defeat. The defenders wallowed in their fallibility and the aberrations were so outlandish that they were virtually a comfort to the new head coach Martin Jol, who could not bring himself to envisage that life will go on like this.

Incredibly, there was no sign of the feast of goals to come in a typically hard-fought but goalless first thirty minutes. Noureddine Naybet then directed a Michael Carrick free-kick past Lehmann 8 minutes before half-time. Cygan nodded over the bar as the interval was approaching and there were seconds left before the interlude when Thierry Henry ran onto Lauren's intelligent pass, beating his man before calmly firing into the Lilywhites' net to level the scores.

Wenger's half-time team talk inspired the visitors to a tremendous offensive onslaught in the second period. Arsenal should have gone in front within a minute of the restart, when Ljungberg crossed the ball low to the far post. The home fans inside White Hart Lane appeared to be in suspended animation waiting for the referee's whistle, but the Spaniard Reyes was the only player to continue. It was unfortunate for him; his anticipation was not as good as his touch on this occasion as the ball appeared to get stuck in his feet, which meant he could only offer a weak poke at the Tottenham 'keeper Paul Robinson.

Lauren, the quiet but tough right-back from Cameroon via Mallorca, put the Gunners ahead from the spot ten minutes after the break. The spot-kick occurred when Ljungberg twisted past Noe Pamarot in the box before the French defender unceremoniously dragged him down. It was reassuring for Gooners in the ground that Lauren struck home from the spot with a confidence that belied the tense and hostile atmosphere emanating from the home stands. It also mirrored the penalty he had scored against Spurs in the double-winning season of 2002 – in terms of netting rather than placement, as his strike that found the net two years earlier had been mishit.

Patrick Vieira was to make it 3-1 with half an hour remaining, matching his efforts seven months prior to this game when he netted on the day Arsenal won the League for the second time at White Hart Lane. The leggy legend vigorously won the ball in midfield and drove forward. With only Robinson to beat, the Gunners captain coolly lifted the ball over the onrushing 'keeper and into the net once Robinson had prematurely committed himself to diving to the right.

The diminutive Spurs forward Jermaine Defoe pulled his team back into the contest with a strike virtually from the restart to make it 3-2, before the effectual Freddie Ljungberg made it 4-2 in the 69th minute. Fabregas won the ball and played a one-two with Henry before sending the ball to Ljungberg, who poked a low shot under Robinson. As Wenger said of Freddie, 'He was very influential in the second half.'

Ledley King's header put Arsenal under pressure again when he nodded in at the near post, but substitute Robert Pires calmed Arsenal fears as he ran onto Henry's intelligent reverse pass; his shot beat a frustrated Robinson at the near post that summed up his club's shambolic defending on the day. Frederic Kanoute's strike with three minutes remaining made it a worrying last few seconds for Wenger, but his team remained defensively steadfast during the frantic finale – something they couldn't be accused of through the majority of the second half. But Arsenal fans didn't mind; a North London derby triumph at the home of their rivals is always to be savoured.

27

Everton (H)

11 May 2005

The 11 May 2005 marked the last occasion in history when Arsenal FC wore red at Highbury. Arsène Wenger's team marked the juncture with a perfect performance in slamming a record seven goals past a David Moyes led Everton, who had just finished in fourth place and Champions League qualification.

In truth, it was a relentless exhibition of high-quality attacking football culminating in a breathless accumulation of goals – all of which were gleefully celebrated by a happy Highbury crowd. They also took the opportunity to remind Wenger not to let the legendary Dennis Bergkamp depart the club just yet through their constant but good-natured chants of 'Sign him up' and 'One more year'. The fans and connoisseurs of good football everywhere were to get their fervent wish only days later as the Dutch master put pen to paper for a further twelve months.

Whether this game had any sway on Wenger's decision is debatable, but what it clear is that Bergkamp was Everton's main tormentor on the night, scoring once and providing assists for three more goals. The timing was appropriate – just like Arsenal the Dutchman was to enjoy one final season at Highbury.

Arsenal: Lehmann, Lauren, Campbell, Senderos, Cole, Pires, Vieira, Edu, Reyes, Bergkamp, Van Persie. Substitutes: Henry for Van Persie, Flamini for Vieira, Fabregas for Pires. Not used: Almunia, Toure.
Everton: Wright, Hibbert, Weir, Yobo, Pistone, Carsley, McFadden, Watson, Arteta, Kilbane, Beattie. Substitutes: Bent for Beattie, Ferguson for Arteta. Not used: Stubbs, Plessis, Turner.
Referee: A. Wiley
Attendance: 38,073

The next morning's *Liverpool Echo* wrote sheepishly,

Everton suffered the club's heaviest defeat in fifty-six years. When the Blues qualified for the Champions League last weekend, it was one of the finest Evertonians have experienced for a decade. The Blues were subjected to an attacking masterclass by Arsène Wenger's flamboyant outfit. It was an open free flowing contest which is tantamount to suicide against a side as skilful and adept as Arsenal.

Arsène Wenger's team achieved their biggest win in the nine years the sophisticated Frenchman had led the club. The result also secured runners-up spot to Chelsea in the penultimate League game of the season.

Dennis Bergkamp set up the first goal of what was to prove an entertaining and eventful night when he crossed for Van Persie to score after only 9 minutes.

'It has been a long time of my career – it is always on your mind but hopefully we can sort something out,' said Bergkamp, who had been at Arsenal since June 1995. Wenger told the press afterwards that he'd made his decision on Bergkamp's future, but wouldn't confirm the answer until a few days later. 'We'll sit down before the end of the season – but I feel it will come out at the end of the season,' Wenger said cryptically before adding, perhaps revealing his inner thoughts on the matter, 'You have to be special to play at 36 at this level – and Dennis is super-special.'

Robert Pires added number two only 120 seconds later rendering the match effectively over with 79 minutes still to play. It was to prove to be a long 79 minutes for Everton, who appeared to be playing as if they had spent the previous week deep in celebration of the fourth-place finish. Pires managed to head the ball over ex-Arsenal 'keeper Richard Wright, who was making his first appearance in three months for the Merseyside outfit.

Bergkamp then set up Vieira for the third 8 minutes before the break. Thierry Henry, who himself was returning to the side after a month out, replaced Van Persie at half-time in a double substitution that saw Flamini come on for Patrick Vieira. The change acted as a prelude for an avalanche of second-half goals. Soon after, it was four when Henry, receiving the ball from Bergkamp, played the ball through to Pires, who finished in style on 50 minutes.

Arsenal's utter dominance carried, although they would have to wait another 20 minutes to add their fifth. The North Londoners were awarded a penalty in the 70th minute after Everton defender Lee Carsley was called for handball. Henry then altruistically gave penalty-taking duties to the Valencia-bound Edu, who netted in what was to be his final game at Highbury. Bergkamp was to crown his performance in the 77th, as he showed great vision and technique in controlling an aerial ball before slotting past a dejected Wright.

Flamini then added Arsenal's seventh and last goal in the 85th minute. The Gunners' dominance was far from over, as German international goalkeeper Jens Lehmann performed a good save to prevent Duncan Ferguson from notching a consolation.

During the 2002/03 season, Everton conceded fourteen goals in three matches against Arsenal. 'I am embarrassed by tonight's performance,' David Moyes, the Everton manager, said afterwards.

Arsenal's performance at that time was the fourth biggest Premiership win.

Arsène Wenger showed dignity in refusing to crow. He showed sympathy with Everton for their sorry night by bearing in mind their excellent fourth-place finish to make it into the next term's Champions League third round qualifying stage. (Which they unfortunately lost to eventual semi-finalists Villarreal 5-1 – who in turn were beaten by Arsenal.)

Wenger said, 'Everton's season is the miracle of the season. They lost Wayne Rooney before the start of the season and then Thomas Gravesen to Real Madrid in January, but it looks like every time you make them bleed they resurrect themselves.'

Yet Wenger and the club were far more concerned with the upcoming FA Cup final in their hunt for silverware than goalscoring records – as enjoyable as they had been.

However, perhaps the last line on the match should go to the *Liverpool Echo*: 'It was Everton's misfortune that they ran into an Arsenal side at the top of their game,' cheekily awarding goalkeeper Wright Man of the Match and stating, 'On a night when he conceded seven, had it not been for his acrobatics it could have been even worse.'

28

Manchester United (N)

21 May 2005

The club finished a distant twelve points behind a José Mourinho-inspired Chelsea on eighty-three points (which would have given them the League by four points in Manchester United's 1998/99 treble-winning season). However, they claimed second spot over third-place United by six points and an impressive twenty-nine more goals scored, as the Gunners ended with eighty-seven strikes to their name. With the runners-up spot secured – thereby avoiding a tricky Champions League qualifying tie that saw a solid fourth-placed Everton side thrashed 5-1 away by rampant Villarreal – the team and the fans could look forward to another FA Cup final trip to Cardiff's Millennium Stadium.

Arsenal started the run to their seventeenth FA Cup final appearance by beating Stoke City 2-1 on 9 January in N5 after being 1-0 down at half-time – the match notable for a certain Emmanuel Eboué's debut in red and white.

The end of the month saw the team dispose of a disappointing Glenn Hoddle-led Wolverhampton Wanders at Highbury in round four. Ljungberg and a Vieira penalty saw off the Black Country side comfortably.

North London witnessed a 1-1 draw (Pires) in the fifth round against Sheffield United, three days before their vital Champions League second round away match with German giants Bayern Munich in the Olympiastadion. A poor 3-1 defeat in Bavaria ensued, which, despite a Thierry Henry winner in a 1-0 victory in the home leg, saw Arsenal eliminated from Europe, leaving the FA Cup as their only realistic chance of silverware. The replay staged at Bramall Lane – in front of their highest crowd of the season, 27,595 – sandwiched as it was between the Euro ties, saw supporters endure a poor game over 120 minutes; the 0-0 stalemate leaving the tie to be settled 4-2 to the travellers on penalties. The spot-kick practice Arsenal gained was to prove to be useful at the season's denouement.

An important 1-0 sixth-round triumph at the Reebok against Bolton Wanders from an early Freddie Ljungberg goal in a lunchtime kick-off – many bleary-eyed Gooners, who made the long trek up the M6 to the North West, missed his third-minute goal – settled the tie. What they did witness was him firing over from 2 yards out in front of an open goal in the latter stages.

But the only thing that mattered was reaching the semi-final, which were held in Cardiff. Against another team from the North West, the Londoners swept Blackburn Rovers aside 3-0 with van Persie netting two late goals to set up a repeat of the heart-breaking 1999 FA Cup semi-final.

Arsenal were out to avenge that crushing defeat and didn't care how they achieved it.

Arsenal: Lehmann, Cole, Toure, Senderos, Lauren, Vieira, Fabregas, Gilberto, Pires, Reyes, Bergkamp. Substitutes: Ljungberg for Bergkamp, van Persie for Fabregas, Edu for Pires. Not used: Almunia, Campbell.
Manchester United: Carroll, Silvestre, Ferdinand, Brown, O'Shea, Scholes, Keane, Fletcher, Ronaldo; Rooney, van Nistelrooy. Substitutes: Fortune for O'Shea, Giggs for Fletcher. Not used: Howard, G. Neville, Smith.
Penalty Shoot-out: van Nistelrooy (scored), Lauren (scored), Scholes (saved), Ljungberg (scored), Ronaldo (scored), van Persie (scored), Rooney (scored), Cole (scored), Keane (scored), Vieira (scored).
Score: 0-0 aet. Arsenal won 5-4 on penalties.
Attendance: 71,876

The FA Cup final took place at the Millennium Stadium, Cardiff, for the fifth successive year due to the laborious rebuilding of the 'new' Wembley. The showpiece of the English domestic season was the fifth meeting between the two adversaries that season. The Gunners lost both League games and a League Cup quarter-final tie at Old Trafford, contested by what was effectively two reserve sides. The only game Arsenal had triumphed that term against the Red Devils was the Community Shield, also held at the Millennium nine months previously, as they prevailed against Sir Alex Ferguson's team 3-1. It would prove to be a good omen.

United sprang two surprises in their starting line-up, with Roy Carroll preferred to Tim Howard in goal and Ryan Giggs left on the bench in favour of Darren Fletcher.

There were eyebrows raised at Wenger's selection of Philippe Senderos ahead of Sol Campbell at centre-half, as the Swiss youngster found himself under early United pressure. Arsenal, missing an injured Thierry Henry, elected for caution over their usual attacking intent.

With Ronaldo beating Lauren on the left flank to cross for Scholes, it was a relief to the estimated 30,000 Arsenal fans who had made the journey along the M4 to see Scholes execute a poor finish, which failed to trouble the scoreline.

Ex-West Ham United centre-half Rio Ferdinand sent the ball into the net just after the 20 minute mark, after German 'keeper Jens Lehmann prevented eventual Man of the Match Wayne Rooney's low shot, but the effort was correctly ruled out for offside by Cup final ref Rob Styles.

Rooney then fired a powerful shot at Lehmann, resulting in the ball being palmed over the bar. It was all United, as Arsenal fans everywhere hoped for a change in fortune. But it was difficult to see how, with Dennis Bergkamp completely isolated on his own up front and the team offering few problems offensively. Wenger, it seemed, had for once compromised his attacking ideals by controversially abandoning his preferred 4-4-2, opting instead for a 4-5-1 tactical formation. Yet at times, even that configuration looked over-optimistic with the shape of the team appearing to switch to an ultra-defensive 5-4-1 when soaking up pressure, with Vieira or the Brazilian Gilberto occasionally acting as auxiliary defenders so deep did they drop.

Yet for all the good form that Rooney showed, the team from Manchester simply couldn't find a way through Wenger's obdurate defence. It was as if the economics graduate from Alsace had morphed into a pragmatic working-class Glaswegian named George Graham.

But the game was never destined to be 1-0 to Arsenal – certainly not during the second half when the North Londoners fought desperately just to stay on level terms.

Still, the pressure from the Mancunians continued. Ronaldo narrowly fired wide from 20 yards out. The man from Madeira was on fire as he gave the consistent Lauren arguably his biggest challenge in an Arsenal shirt. Vieira's old adversary Roy Keane could have killed the match (or at least put the majority watching in the ground and at home out of their misery) on 85 minutes. Ironically, his bitter rival, who 'came from Senegal/and played for Arsenal', somehow managed to successfully attempt a vital block after Lehmann had miscalculated a Ronaldo corner and spilled the ball.

Yet as the game wore on through extra time, the feeling started to grow that Arsenal's durability prompted by Arsène Wenger's unusual pragmatism could see a famous smash and grab raid – even when José Reyes received a second yellow card in the dying seconds of the game and gained the unwanted distinction of becoming only the second player to be sent off in an FA Cup final.

As Styles blew the whistle on 120 minutes of stalemate, the realisation dawned that this would be the first-ever FA Cup final to be settled on penalties.

Van Nistelrooy and Lauren emphatically scored in the rain, with Lauren's relief getting the better of him by celebrating in front of the United fans. However, the normally collected Scholes betrayed his nerves by taking an unnecessarily long run up, hitting the ball low to Lehmann's right. Fortunately for Arsenal, the dependable German chose the correct side to parry, even if you wouldn't have guessed it by his utterly unruffled reaction. Both Ljungberg and Ronaldo sent Carroll and Jens the wrong way to make it 2-2, and both van Persie and Rooney struck confident penalties, with Cole also netting his. It was down to the old warrior Roy Keane to keep United in the game. It was no surprise he did.

With the tension now unbearable at 4-4, and only Patrick Vieira left to take one, it was instructive that the two great rivals Vieira and Keane passed each other on the lonely walk from penalty spot to centre circle. Neither said a word to each other, but everyone knew how they felt. If Vieira emulated Keane in successfully scoring his kick, Arsenal would win the FA Cup. With the rest of the Arsenal team huddled in the centre circle, with their arms draped over one another, they watched as a unified band of brothers, along with the hordes of nervous Gooners in the ground and tens of millions of Arsenal fans worldwide.

Among a backdrop of boos, Vieira, with what was to be his last-ever kick for Arsenal FC, scored his penalty with a low, powerful shot, which evaded Carroll's despairing dive. It was fitting that the Arsenal midfield legend ran straight to Jens Lehmann while the rest of the team made a mad dash to join them.

Arsenal had won their tenth FA Cup in a performance that had United fans moaning about their defensive play. But the team, the club and the supporters simply did not care. Nor did Arsène Wenger, who said in an honest estimation of the day, 'At the start, I didn't set up like that and suddenly Manchester United were all over us and I realised that physically we were not able to compete, so I said, "OK let's defend as long as we can."'

For much-loved and subsequently much-missed Patrick Vieira, who played his last game in an Arsenal shirt that day in Cardiff, lifting the trophy was all that mattered.

29

Middlesbrough (H)
14 January 2006

The previous few games had been a mixed bag for Arsène Wenger. The last two League matches had finished 0-0, away at Aston Villa on New Year's Eve, and home to Manchester United in the first game of 2006 four days later. Given his team's propensity for attacking football, this was a state of affairs virtually unheard of.

Wenger maintained, 'We wanted to win against Manchester United but it was a high pace game and I felt both teams were always trying to have a break to get the other on the counter-attack,' before adding ominously, 'We can still improve but the team is on a good way at the moment.'

Cardiff City had been dispatched 2-1 (Pires 2) in what was to be the last-ever FA Cup tie at dear old Highbury. Wigan Athletic had then beaten the Londoners' League cup side 1-0 in the north-west in the first leg of the Carling Cup semi-final, days before the visitors from Teeside travelled south. Ironically, the goal was scored by Austrian debutant and self-confessed Arsenal fan Paul Scharner.

However, Saturday 14 January 2006 would bring a large helping of cheer to Wenger and any Highbury faithful suffering January blues, and leave Middlesbrough shell-shocked – proving he was right to say his team was in a 'good way at the moment'.

Arsenal: Lehmann, Lauren, Cygan, Senderos, Djourou, Silva, Fabregas, Pires, Ljungberg, Reyes, Henry. Substitutes: Cole for Cygan, Flamini for Silva, Hleb for Pires. Not used: Almunia, Lupoli.
Middlesbrough: Jones, Riggott, Bates, Taylor, Parnaby, Rochemback, Mendieta, Doriva, Morrison, Yakubu, Viduka. Substitutes: Wheater for Taylor, Johnson for Viduka, Cattermole for Rochemback. Not used: Schwarzer, Hasselbaink.
Referee: Rob Styles
Attendance: 38,186

As Matt Scott of *The Guardian* wrote prophetically in his match report on this sublime Gunners performance,

> If there is one thing more troubling than Sven-Göran Eriksson's latest indiscretion, it is that Steve McClaren is currently the man most likely to succeed him as England's manager. It was a merciless Arsenal, spearheaded by a reinvigorated Thierry Henry, that shredded McClaren's callow team but that does not mitigate the Middlesbrough manager's lack of ideas and invention.

Steve McClaren had said in mitigation, 'With the young and inexperienced back four we had it was always going to be difficult.' Yet Wenger's starting back four included a callow Johan Djourou, making his League debut alongside Philippe Senderos, in only his eighteenth Premiership start, with the erratic Pascal Cygan being played out of position at left-back.

McClaren also added, 'I've been to Highbury with good teams and conceded goals', as if that were a decent excuse.

Wenger, who made five changes from the side that lost to Wigan for his part simply stated afterwards, 'We won 7-0 but we could have scored a lot more.'

Thierry Henry's hat-trick was good enough for starters on a day when he made it 150 League goals and counting in Arsenal colours. It was a number that also matched legendary Gunners star from the 1930s Cliff Bastin and his sixty-year club record.

A modest Henry said,

I didn't step on the pitch thinking I wanted to beat Bastin's record I just wanted to help the team and it was great to be on the end of some brilliant moves. All of the records are good but it's more important that we go on a good run to finish in the top four. That is vital that we finish in the top four. It's vital for me, for the club and for the fans. It's vital for everyone.

Rob Hughes, writing in *The Sunday Times* the following day, said,

The problem with being Thierry Daniel Henry is that one day soon they are going to pull down Highbury, and there won't be any records left for him to eclipse … it is about grace, it is about timing, it is about a ridiculous degree of skill and performance.

Henry warmed Gunners fans on a grey, dank but, in terms of the result, far from dismal mid-winter's afternoon by opening the scoring with a tremendous volley on 20 minutes. Before 'Boro had time to regroup, it was 2-0, with Philippe Senderos guiding a powerful header past Jones before Henry raced clear of the Teesiders' static defence to slam home his second of the game. Robert Pires then lobbed the unfortunate Jones with an audacious chip, which left Gilberto Silva to calmly head home the fifth, before Henry struck his record-equalling third to joyous acclaim from all four corners of the venerable ground. To compound matters for Middlesbrough, McClaren and the away fans at Highbury, Doriva was deservedly sent off for a second yellow, which left Alexander Hleb to complete the scoring and make it a hugely satisfying 7-0 to Arsenal with a simple tap in as the visitors on and off the pitch prayed for the final whistle.

Wenger said afterwards,

We played our game and the goals came as a consequence of the quality of our game. Of course, Thierry scored three – and everybody nearly scored! But Reyes contributed with his final balls and the most important thing is that the team plays the game we want to play and plays with a great spirit.

A stunned Middlesbrough boss Steve McClaren said, 'This has been my toughest day as Middlesbrough manager without a shadow of a doubt.'

The Middlesbrough website described proceedings as 'an afternoon when Arsenal turned on a master-class, Thierry Henry equalled an all-time record, 'Boro suffered their heaviest ever Premiership defeat and had a man sent-off'. The bare facts making it hard to imagine a more depressing summation from a 'Boro viewpoint.

However, from an Arsenal viewpoint, it was a magnificent afternoon's work. The fact that Wenger in his post-match press conference let slip that Southampton starlet Theo Walcott was to be signed imminently was a bonus.

As Hughes in the *Sunday Times* perceptively noted ahead of the youngster's arrival, 'The Arsenal team has been built around Henry, has relied on his inspiration, and been too over reliant on playing for the role designed around him. There could be change on the way.'

And early the next week after, the sixteen-year-old put pen to paper for Arsenal, Wenger proclaimed, 'We are delighted Theo has signed for the Club and will make a fantastic addition to our squad.'

Walcott himself stated,

I'm so pleased to be joining Arsenal, a club I have admired for a long time. Coming to Arsenal will give me the opportunity to work with world class players every day and play football at the highest possible level.

30

Real Madrid (A)

21 February 2006

Arsène Wenger had repeatedly used the word 'belief' in his pre-match press conference in Madrid prior to this momentous game at Real's citadel, the iconic and intimidating Bernabeu. 'Belief and defensive solidity' were the two pillars that he clung to as Arsenal went into the tie as huge underdogs against an in-form team packed with Galácticos in a stadium where no English team had triumphed before.

Wenger had also suggested to the press in the Spanish capital beforehand a win could act as a springboard to lift his team to further heights in the League, struggling as they were adrift of fourth place that February.

It would be hard to imagine how many of the 3,500 travelling fans, packed high up in the away end, with another 3,000 estimated to be dotted around the ground, having bought their black market tickets in the bars and restaurants of the Plaza Mayor earlier in the day, had actually believed their team could win.

In the end, Wenger had been proved correct. Belief and defensive solidity were vital. He simply forgot to mention the final component: having Thierry Henry on your team.

Real Madrid: Casillas, Cicinho, Sergio, Woodgate, Carlos, Gravesen, Beckham, Guti, Zidane, Robinho, Ronaldo. Substitutes: Mejia for Woodgate, Julio Baptista for Gravesen, Raul for Robinho. Not used: Cobeno, Salgado, Cassano, Diogo.
Arsenal: Lehmann, Eboue, Toure, Senderos, Flamini, Ljungberg, Hleb, Silva, Fabregas, Reyes, Henry. Substitutes: Pires for Hleb, Song for Fabregas, Diaby for Reyes. Not used: Almunia, Walcott, Djourou, Lupoli.
Referee: Stefano Farina (Italy)
Attendance: 80,000

The Real Madrid team that started against Arsenal contained such world-renowned and world-class figures as Zinedine Zidane, Roberto Carlos, the Brazilian Ronaldo, Robinho, Iker Casillas in goal and David Beckham. But the bravery and doggedness Arsenal showed against such blue-blood thoroughbreds has never been forgotten. Along with Thierry Henry's attacking masterclass.

The Guardian's Matt Scott wrote in his match report,

Maturity of the performances of Gilberto, Thierry Henry and Freddie Ljungberg ensured Arsenal could dominate the most venerable club in European football ... there was genuine backbone to the spine of Arsenal's side and belief.

Arsène Wenger's under-strength squad performed with great reliability, maturity and attacking flair in the opening period. They could even have gone in at the break a couple of goals to the good.

It took a decent one-handed save from Casillas to stop the Gunners netting in the opening exchanges as Henry released Reyes in the second minute. Madrid then lost the injury-prone Jonathan Woodgate in under 10 minutes as he hobbled off after pulling his hamstring. Roberto Carlos then performed a superbly timed tackle to save his team as Arsenal attacked again with Henry, the chief architect, again feeding Freddie Ljungberg, who skipped past Casillas but was denied by the veteran Brazilian just as he shaped to score. The Arsenal fans high up in the gods and around the stadium simply couldn't believe the mastery they were exhibiting over the muchlauded home team. Henry himself could and should have put the North Londoners ahead after just 9 minutes when he escaped his marker and leapt to nod a Reyes' cross, just past the post.

Real finally woke up on 26 minutes, when the legendary Zinedine Zidane's crossed for David Beckham to head wide. The England captain and global style icon also squandered an easy chance on 32 minutes as Ronaldo won the ball from a ponderous Philippe Senderos to put Beckham away, but Jens Lehmann was quick to sense the danger and smothered the threat.

Many in the ground were still finishing their half-time *jamon* and *rioja* when Arsenal and Henry strode out purposely for the second half. The majority of lucky souls who witnessed what happened next can tell their grandchildren they saw one of the best goals ever scored in either the Champions League or its predecessor, the European Cup.

Henry picked up the ball in the middle of the pitch from a Fabregas pass and drove past four different challenges – holding off Ronaldo, easing past Mejia and Guti, and muscling past Sergio Ramos, who he tormented all night – while running at top speed. Entering the box, he drew the angle from Casillas before executing a stunning left-foot finish. His impossibly cool celebration as he ran to the corner, far beneath the bulk of the away support, succeeded in drawing the many Gooners scattered around the ground, deep in enemy territory, to their feet. It was an incredible moment and an incredible goal.

Wenger said, 'It was an exceptional goal – for me it was top, top, top class. We had Thierry Henry at the very peak of his game. Thierry scored after a pass from Fabregas – things don't change!'

the Gunners offered stout resistance to the expected Real revival. Within six minutes of Raul replacing an ineffective Robinho, he almost pulled Madrid back into the game with header from Beckham's free-kick that he flicked narrowly wide.

Yet Wenger's team were still dangerous on the break, with substitute Abou Diaby nearly crowning his appearance with a goal with a minute remaining. Casillas saved at the Frenchman's feet before a Beckham cross just failed to see a leveller from Ronaldo after five minutes injury time – but to the relief of Wenger and his team, the Brazilian failed to connect with the Englishman's tantalising cross.

As the final whistle went, Arsenal celebrated what was an amazing victory – one that would always be remembered as their fans sang 'Adios' lustily to the stunned home support as they slid away into the Madrid night.

The Gunners became the first English team to beat Madrid away at the Bernabeu. The 1-0 triumph was also part of their ten-game run of successive clean sheets in the Champions League that took Wenger's men all the way to the final that season.

Wenger said afterwards,

> That was when I started to think this team could win the Champions League. I knew that
> we were on the way to delivering something special and I was very confident before the
> game at Real Madrid. Knowing that they had Zidane, Beckham, Ronaldo, Raul, Robinho
> – they had an unbelievable offensive potential. We went there with people who had no
> experience at the top level. We had Emmanuel Eboue and Kolo Toure at the back with
> Philippe Senderos and Mathieu Flamini, as well as a very young Cesc Fabregas. You have
> to have a good defence if you want to win the Champions League. I believe that it is an
> amazing achievement. I feel we have grown as a team during these last two months.

As the headline in the notable Spanish newspaper Diaro AS read the next morning: 'Henry
was the galactico – Ronaldo was invisible.'

Henry, for his part, received a standing ovation when he stepped onto the plane taking
the team back to London. Team player that he was, he stated modestly and with caution, 'It
was a great night but we need to keep our feet on the ground and not get carried away.'

Alvaro Mejia reflecting his side's impotence against an unstoppable Henry moaned
in admiration,

> We did everything to try and stop him. We tried to push him, pull him and we tried to kick
> him. Nothing worked. I've never seen anything like it. Henry is their main man and one of
> the greats in Europe.

After Arsenal shut out Madrid in the return in London two weeks later to win the tie 1-0 on
aggregate, a gracious David Beckham said, 'We wanted a few and could not get them. But
overall I wish them luck – they are a good team. Thierry Henry is a special player.'

Arsène Wenger and captain Tony Adams proudly hold the Premiership Trophy and FA Cup in 2002. (*Courtesy of Press Association*)

Emirates Stadium. (*Courtesy of Darkensyva Flickr*)

Arsenal's head coach Arsène Wenger reacts during the UEFA Champions League match between Bayern Munich and Arsenal in Munich, Germany, 11 March 2014. (*Courtesy of Press Association*)

Arsène Wenger, center right, and captain Thomas Vermaelen, center left, hold up the trophy to the supporters outside the Emirates Stadium at the end of their parade on a open top bus through the street of London in celebration of their FA Cup win, Sunday 18 May 2014. (*Courtesy of Press Association*)

Nacho Monreal of Arsenal and Arsène Wenger during the UEFA Champions League *v.* Borussia Dortmund on 6 November 2013 at the Signal Iduna Park Stadium in Dortmund, Germany. (*Courtesy of Press Association*)

31

Juventus (H)

28 March 2006

The previous matches in this fixture contained drama and excitement. From the last-gasp winner in Turin, by the tragic Paul Vaessen in 1980, to the comprehensive dismantling of Juve 3-1 at an atmospheric Highbury late in 2001, matches between these two giants invariably produced a spectacle.

This game was no different. Against a side that was to contain the nucleus of the Italian 2006 World Cup-winning team only a few months later, Arsène Wenger's men were simply outstanding. Therefore, it was somewhat ironic that in the build-up to this eagerly awaited tie, the considerable presence of ex-Arsenal legend Patrick Vieira loomed large. Yet by the end of this gripping, pulsating – and for Wenger and Arsenal fans – hugely satisfying performance and result, the name of a younger, far more diminutive player was on everybody's lips, someone who was now talked about as Vieira's heir apparent: Cesc Fabregas.

In the pre-match press conference, Wenger talked presciently of the Champions League fast-tracking youngsters saying,

> I am convinced this Arsenal team is on the way. But you cannot afford to waste time in this job. That is why we have to be in the Champions League next season. This team is so young that they could gain three or four years by being in the Champions League.

For nineteen-year-old Fabregas, his performance against La Vecchia Signora was a sure sign he was on the right track.

Arsenal: Lehmann, Eboue, Toure, Senderos, Flamini, Hleb, Silva, Fabregas, Pires, Henry, Reyes. Substites: Van Persie (82) for Reyes. Not used: Almunia, Diaby, Bergkamp, Song, Walcott, Djourou.
Juventus: Buffon, Zebina, Thuram, Cannavaro, Zambrotta, Camoranesi, Vieira, Emerson, Mutu, Ibrahimovic, Trezeguet. Substitues: Chiellini for Mutu, Zalayeta for Tezeguet. Not used: Abbiati, Kovac, Balzaretti, Blasi, Giannichedda.
Referee: Peter Frojdfeldt
Attendance: 35,472

This game provided another magical night in the Wenger era – and certainly one of the most enjoyable.

Matt Dickinson, chief football correspondent of *The Times,* wrote in his match report,

They produced the last rites on Real Madrid's ageing Galácticos and last night Arsenal's young guns appeared to usher another group of celebrated names towards retirement. Dashing and daring, Arsène Wenger's mesmerising XI all but handed the pensioners's bus passes to the shamefaced representatives of the Old Lady of Turin.

　　Italian reporters were as breathless as Emerson and Vieira as they tried to come to terms with the beating inflicted on the runaway Serie A leaders.

It was instructive to learn that Arsenal's back four cost £5 million – Juventus' outgoings a staggering £100 million. Yet it was Arsenal who kept another clean sheet in their burgeoning Champions League run that had already eclipsed Czech Champions Sparta Prague, beaten Ajax in Amsterdam, triumphed against the Galácticos in Madrid – and now this.

Wenger's men started the game on fire. They were energetic, and their dynamism resulted in a high tempo so unsettling to the ageing stars of Serie A it was easy to agree with Wenger's post-match assertion that 'my only regret is that we did not score more'.

As it was the Gunners' determination to win shone through – along with their power, confidence and passing ability and movement off the ball. The inspired football was a joy to watch. The fans knew it was going to be a special night from the moment Robert Pires beat ex-Highbury icon Vieira to a header.

The double act of Pires and young Fabregas provided the first real chance of the game on 16 minutes as they linked up to force a shot. As Pires chested down a throw in, he spied his young colleague running through. The Frenchman then sent a sublime backheel, which sent Cesc through on goal. If the way he snatched at the chance was unfortunate, he would more than make up for it shortly afterwards.

And if Toure disposing Trezuguet before he could send Ibrahimovic through brought thunderous acclaim, perhaps the defining moment of such a masterful performance that had the Highbury crowd singing 'There's Only One Arsène Wenger' lustily and reverentially came in the 40th minute.

With ex-Highbury colossus Vieira embarking on another one of his driving runs for Juve, it was Pires of all people who stopped him in his tracks with an unlikely sliding tackle, which was greeted with as loud a roar by the Highbury faithful as if it were a goal. To add to their incredulity, Pires then scuttled forward before feeding Henry. Arsenal's record goalscorer still had significant work to help his side find a way past Lillian Thuram, his teammate in France's 1998 World Cup-winning squad, Fabio Cannavaro, who was to captain Italy to the World months later and achieve the rare feat of a defender winning World Player of the Year by the year's end, and the hugely experienced Gigi Buffon in goal. Yet Henry found a way as he spotted Fabregas running into the box and played a perfect through ball to him.

As Matt Dickinson wrote, 'Fabregas proved that special is in his repertoire. A drop of the shoulder to create some room and a low, placed shot through Thuram's legs sent Highbury into raptures.'

Arsenal continued to overrun the shell-shocked Italians with their vibrant, forceful attacks, and after Buffon had repelled further attempts from Henry and Fabregas again, in the 69th minute his goal was breached for the second occasion that night.

Effortless interchanges between Hleb and Fabregas saw a thoughtful ball played into young Cesc. He would have been forgiven for shooting, but showing the vision that was to become his trademark, he squared the ball to Henry. With Buffon wrong-footed, Henry was simply left with an open goal to pass into.

An utterly miserable night for Juventus was sealed with the complete loss of discipline as Camoranesi and Zebina were justly sent off to complete a searing humiliation for the Italian giants.

As Wenger said afterwards,

We have to keep our feet on the ground and keep our football simple. That is what the boys do and they can do better. They are not inhibited. There is quality in this team and they are good to watch. I believe we will finish the job in the second leg in Italy but there is still a lot to come. It wasn't my target tonight to justify selling Patrick.

With momentum building in the run-in for fourth and a potential Champions League semi-final and final to come, Wenger added,

The win against Real Madrid may have helped us but football is fragile. You have to be cautious. One unexpected defeat and you are back again.

I felt there was one more goal in the game for us. I'm very happy with the performance of the team and the togetherness. There was also fluency and speed and the technical quality was very high in patches.

Juventus boss Fabio Capello, refusing to give any credit whatsoever to an outstanding Arsenal performance, responded by saying somewhat misguidedly, 'The tie is still alive and my team need a big game in Turin.'

It wasn't. And they didn't. A superbly marshalled 0-0 draw saw Wenger's team marching on as another chapter was added to dramatic Arsenal-Juventus matches.

32

Wigan Athletic (H)

7 May 2006

There are certain days, rare days, when everything clicks. When everything goes to plan and all your hopes are realised. This magical day, which saw Highbury stage its last game, was one of those days.

The afternoon saw the final match take place at the club's spiritual home before embarking on the short move down Gillespie Road across Drayton Park to Ashburton Grove and the Emirates. The day was tinged with sadness at the move along with excitement at the prospect of inhabiting a 60,000 stadium up there with the world's best.

But the day would also be remembered for the frantic race for fourth place and vital Champions League qualification. This was required not only to keep and attract the best players to the club, but also to keep money flowing into the coffers in order to fund the new stadium. The thought of missing out on qualification and the many positives associated with it were too horrible to contemplate. The fact that it was Spurs, who were fighting the Gunners for that cherished fourth spot, made the day even more gripping.

Never mind the small matter of the forthcoming Champions League final against Barcelona in Paris the following week, all that mattered on the day was leaving Highbury with a win to see off the ground in style – and to clinch Champions League football.

Quite simply, with Spurs starting the day in the coveted fourth position, Arsenal had to better Tottenham's result at West Ham to pip their deadly rivals to a Champions League spot.

What was to unfold saw one of the most dramatic and memorable afternoons in Highbury's long existence.

Arsenal: Lehmann, Eboue, Toure, Campbell, Cole, Hleb, Fabregas, Gilberto, Pires, Reyes, Henry. Substitutes: Ljungberg for Pires, Bergkamp for Reyes, van Persie for Hleb. Not used: Almunia, Djourou.
Wigan: Pollitt, Chimbonda, Jackson, Scharner, Baines, Thompson, Kavanagh, Ziegler, McCulloch, Roberts, Camara. Substitutes: Francis for Ziegler, Johansson for Thompson, Connolly for Camara. Not used: Henchoz, Wright.
Referee: Uriah Rennie (S. Yorkshire)
Attendance: 38,359

Matt Hughes in *The Times* wrote,

Arsenal celebrated qualification for next season's competition as if they had won the Champions League, which they may well do in nine days time, the only possible way of eclipsing a remarkable end to the season. Having predicted a party, Arsène Wenger's side gave this proud old stadium the raucous send-off it deserved.

On a day of farewells, it was fitting that Robert Pires, the dashing wide-man who had been the architect of so many goals, opened the scoring on eight minutes ahead of his move to Villarreal on a two-year contract curiously denied to him at Arsenal.

With all ears pressed to radios and many eyes flitting between the pitch and mobile phone updates, Wigan, who had largely been forgotten in the build-up – save for the nice touch by the club to provide their travelling fans with a free t-shirt to make the game, complementing the 35,000 red-and-white ones laid out on every home seat in the stadium – equalised through Paul Scharner. More excruciating drama was to come as David Thompson netted from the penalty spot to put the Latics 2-1 ahead after Sol Campbell appeared to drag back Jason Roberts in the box.

Fortunately, the lead only lasted two minutes, as Henry scored his first of the day. Not long after the start of the second period came the glorious news that old foe Teddy Sheringham had missed a penalty at Upton Park. Moments later, Henry benefitted from a Thompson mistake, slotting home to make it 3-2, meaning Arsenal were now ahead in the game and the League table. Both leads were not to be relinquished again that day.

King Henry completed his hat-trick from the penalty spot on 76 minutes. Overcome by emotion, among the maelstrom of delirium on and off the pitch, he showed his class and poise by slowly kneeling down and kissing the Highbury turf in supplication and celebration. All that was left was for Spurs to capitulate at Upton Park, conveniently using food poisoning as an excuse. Once news filtered through to Highbury of West Ham's second goal to make it 2-1, with a matter of minutes remaining, the Highbury crowd erupted into spontaneous joy. Spurs' pitiful excuses were soon to be mocked unmercifully on social media. It was that kind of day.

The final minutes can only be described as a mixture of excitement, latent tension at the fear of their rivals scoring two late, and highly unlikely goals joy, celebration and a touch of regret at the thought of never watching a game at Highbury again. Rennie blew the final whistle on the 2,010th and final match at Arsenal Stadium as the famous old timepiece on the Clock End showed 4.54 p.m. West Ham were confirmed as beating the Lilywhites, who had also proved nothing but being lily-livered on the day in their weakness to ride out their apparent dicky tummies.

The Arsenal fans assembled in the ground, in the bars and pubs of North London, and everywhere else on the planet, all launched into the mother of all parties as unrestrained festivities began, coupled with no little emotion. (Incidentally a weakness of spirit was exhibited by N17-bound Pascal Chimbonda, who handed in a transfer request in the away team dressing room still clad in full Wigan kit – and gloves.)

The Sun's headline read: 'Gutcha.'

The first Gunner ever to score on the hallowed Highbury turf was Henry King in the 2-1 win against Leicester Fosse in September 1913. Ninety-three years later, King Henry was the last.

Le Roi de Highbury said,

That was the perfect send-off. We are fourth in the league and the table does not lie after thirty-eight games, so we deserve to be in this position. We've missed so many players this season and we did it the hard way. When I kissed the ground after my third, I was saying goodbye to this stadium.

A proud Wenger said,

For the history of the club and for this building here, to finish on a high I am very proud. We would all have felt guilty to have walked out of here on a low after what has happened here for years. There was fantastic excitement, strength of character and quality as well. It is cruel for Tottenham – but sport can be cruel. We have shown so much character.

As Wenger recalled with much fondness later on,

I remember that day very well. Basically Tottenham had to lose at West Ham and we had to win the game. It was a fantastic finish because I thought it would be an absolute shame to spoil the memory of the last day of Highbury.

It was perfect, like a written script. That was absolutely exceptional. It was a day I'll never forget. It was very emotional to leave Highbury. Sometimes I still drive down the road just to go past the old East Stand because it was such a great place and there was so much soul there. It's just special and you don't really know why. Maybe for me, it's because a special part of my life happened there. It is a warm and welcoming place where, on top of that, I have special memories. Everything there was special.

33

Barcelona (N)

17 May 2006

Arsène Wenger was in playful mood when he had the honour of leading the first team to represent the capital in the build-up to the fiftieth Champions League/European Cup final. Having endured a difficult season, he had clinched fourth place after Highbury's memorable last-ever match.

Wenger playfully joshed with the world's reporters in the days leading up to the final in Paris saying,

You thought I was crazy when I said we could win the Champions League this year – and I still am!

We were out of the championship race very early – maybe subconsciously we have chosen this competition this season. I felt in the Champions League we had a good start, concentration was fully there, and we had the potential as well. If you are in there every year, then some years will go better for you than others.

In what would be Arsenal's sixth European final, the mighty Barcelona stood in their way. Yet the team had not conceded a goal for an incredible ten Champions League games, knocking out Real Madrid and Juventus in the process.

Wegner commented,

Barcelona are the super-favourites and we are the dangerous outsider. But I feel that if we play our natural game we are a super-dangerous outsider.

My job is just to get the team to play at their best, just have a real go and I am convinced we would do that. Like many finals, so long as nobody scores, the match will be quite locked because of the importance of the competition.

Once one team scores, though, it will then certainly be an open and crazy game.

It certainly was.

Barcelona: Valdes, Oleguer, Edmilson, van Bronckhorst, Puyol, Marquez, Giuly, Van Bommel, Deco, Eto'o, Ronaldinho. Substitutes: Larsson for Van Bommel, Belletti for Oleguer. Not used: Jorquera, Motta, Xavi, Sylvinho.
Arsenal: Lehmann; Eboue, Toure, Campbell, Cole, Hleb, Gilberto, Fabregas, Pires, Ljungberg, Henry. Substitutes: Almunia for Pires, Flamini for Fabregas, Reyes for Hleb. Not used: Bergkamp, Van Persie, Senderos, Clichy.

Referee: Terje Hauge (Norway)
Attendance: 79,500

Matt Dickinson, chief football correspondent for *The Times,* wrote in admiration after the game,

> Whatever language they speak and wherever they come from, everyone in football understands what is meant by the Spirit of Istanbul. And, as thunder and lightning roared and cracked over the Stade de France, it not only struck twice but consumed both European Cup finalists.
>
> If the phrase equates to heroic defiance, it can also be said to encapsulate the very best of the losers. For the second year running, an English club had graced the biggest stage in continental football with a spirit that refused to die. Reduced to ten men by Jens Lehmann's early dismissal, Arsenal showed all of Liverpool's courage and resolve. It brought them great credit but it couldn't quite secure them the cup.

Arsenal's odyssey to the Champions League final was a story of superb defending, youthful innocence, dramatic bravery, cool temperaments and huge amounts of glorious attacks and memorable goals. These qualities were again shown on a vivid and extraordinary Paris night at the stylish Stade de France. Unfortunately for Arsène Wenger and his ten-man team, who performed heroics on the evening with the iconic jug-eared trophy in sight, they cruelly met their match in a formidable Barca comeback.

Yet Wenger's men could be immensely proud of their efforts, having played a man short for 72 minutes after Jens Lehmann was sent off.

Ronaldinho sent Eto'o through with a clever ball against an Arsenal back line, which was too square. The Cameroon international ran on, skipping past Jens Lehmann, only to see his trailing leg taken by German 'keeper. The ball squirmed onto Giuly's path, who slotted it the gaping net.

Amid the mayhem and uncertainty, referee Terje Hauge had actually blown for the initial foul by Lehmann. Signalling play to be brought back for a free-kick right on the line of the penalty area, the referee also sent Lehmann off for a professional foul. However disappointing the moment was, it was the correct decision and Arsenal knew it in their hearts. The thirty-six-year-old German revealed his emotions by holding his head in his hands – as did many fans in the ground – as he held the unwanted distinction of being the first man to be sent off in such a final.

Lehmann conceded gracefully afterwards, 'He could have given advantage to Barcelona but the referee had to make a very quick decision.'

Wenger added, 'I don't think Jens is a lot to blame for us losing, no.'

It was a painful moment given Lehmann had contributed so much to the club's Champions League cup run. Another man who did was Almunia, who came on for the unlucky Pires, sadly resulting in the exciting winger's last moment in an Arsenal shirt. His service deserved better, but Wenger never hid from the decision – nor his insistence that football can be a cruel game.

The red card was to be a defining moment in the game. But first Arsenal showed their undoubted mettle, refusing to let the dismissal knock them out of their stride. Eboue galloped down Barca's left flank, ending only in an embarrassing dive after a challenge by Puyol. Yet the referee failed to spot it and awarded a free-kick. Perhaps the footballing gods had been annoyed with Puyol's unseemly desperation to get Lehmann sent off and wanted to make amends.

Whatever the reason, Henry, quick to sense the danger area, fired in a free-kick that saw Sol Campbell ghost ahead of Oleguer to skim a powerful header past Valdes at the far post. The 21,000 Arsenal fans in the ground could barely believe that their beloved club was 1-0 in the Champions League final.

Stories abounded of increasingly desperate attempts to gain entry prior to the match. One of the best was a Welsh Gooner who bought a ticket from a dubious source for £500 only to find himself sitting next to Pierre van Hooijdonk and a free bar.

Yet as Campbell said ruefully in an interview with the author for the *Gooner* fanzine many years later, 'I would have happily given up the goal to someone else if it had meant we could have won 1-0.'

Alas, it was not to be. Barcelona attacked as unremittingly as the Parisian hard rain fell. What also fell was the Gunners' attempt to achieve an eleventh successive clean sheet.

As *The Independent*'s Sam Wallace wrote,

They have talked about the weight of history at Highbury all season and last night Arsenal stood on the brink of writing one more remarkable chapter. But against the greatest attacking team in the world, in the European Cup final, the assassination took place in the space of four minutes – and when they struck Barcelona were brutal.

Frank Rijkaard's inspired substitutions in bringing first Henrik Larsson then Juliano Belletti changed the game, leaving the question: have two such changes ever made more of an impact in such a high-profile final?

Yet it was a chance moments before, with the score still at 1-0 to Arsenal, that had many fans and players wondering what might have been.

Henry scampered onto Hleb's through ball only for him to produce a tame shot that Valdes gratefully pounced on. It was the decisive moment for Arsenal in a match of many. Soon after, Larsson's first touch cut Arsenal wide open for Eto'o to slam past Almunia at his near post on 76 minutes – the first goal that they had conceded in almost 1,000 minutes of top-level Champions League football. Then the Gunners, finally reeling under the toil of having to play such a high tempo game with ten men, succumbed to the killer blow from the second substitute. Larsson was once again the creator, this time providing fellow sub Belletti with the chance to fire a low shot in off Almunia to leave many Arsenal fans in tears.

Former Arsenal defender Lee Dixon said,

It seemed to be Wenger's destiny to go and win the trophy this year, but it wasn't to be. But he's got to be so proud of his team tonight. They've been heroic, all of them, and the fact that they've had 10 men, they should be very proud of themselves.

The Sun's headline simply read, 'Barc de Triomphe'.

Wenger himself said,

The referee made a big mistake at a crucial moment – their first goal was offside. The way we lost is very difficult to take because we played fantastically, like we have the whole European season. But in the final, people only remember the team that has won.

I thought we could hang on and I knew nerves would play a part in their game as time went on. They did not look especially dangerous. I was confident because I know we can defend well against their style of passing. The fatigue factor was always there but they did not force us into a position where we really had to defend with their creative play. We were quite comfortable. It was more a question of concentration. We have plenty of good young players behind this team and I would like to thank them all because they have been fantastic. We fought fantastically – it was a great achievement from the team to play ten against eleven against a good side.

The dream was over – but what a journey it was.

34

Aston Villa (H)

19 August 2006

The opening game of any season is significant, but this match against Aston Villa was a hugely symbolic moment in the history of Arsène Wenger's tenure – not to mention the annals of the long and illustrious history of the Arsenal FC.

For the game marked the first competitive match at the newly built Emirates Stadium, and the commencement of the Emirates era.

At the end of the previous decade, the club had decided that evocative, atmospheric, homely Highbury, with a capacity of 38,000, was too small to match the ambitions of the board and Wenger to make Arsenal into a domestic, European and global powerhouse.

Arsenal and Wenger had to learn to balance budgets more than ever as funds were diverted to building the £390 million project, which took 123 weeks to build and finished on time and within budget. It was an incredibly bold step to take and one for which the club visionaries and Wenger himself should be lauded.

As Wenger proudly said on the eve of this game,

> The new stadium project provoked a lot of discussions and debate at board level. We spoke about how far we could go, how unpredictable it would be, how risky it was for the club. Can we put the club in danger for this? So when it finally happened, it was a bit of a dream turning into a reality. You couldn't really believe it.
>
> I'm not a guy who looks back too much. You have to survive and deal with the challenge you have taken. You know that in the history of the club, that will be an important moment where the club moves forward. Some clubs that still have to do it will suffer later. For us it was vital. The landscape of English football has changed in the last 10 years. Today, we could not survive being at Highbury anymore.

The stadium was to be initially labelled 'Ashburton Grove' before Emirates airline bought the naming rights in a fifteen-year sponsorship deal, which included an eight-year shirt deal that was to be worth £100 million in total. The money was a godsend to the cash-strapped Gunners at the time, even if many hardcore fans still refuse to call the new ground anything other than 'Ashburton Grove', or more simply 'The Grove'.

The stadium's first game was actually on 22 July 2006 when it played host to Dennis Bergkamp's testimonial match between Arsenal and Ajax Amsterdam. The match would see Arsenal triumph 2-1, with Ajax's Klaas-Jan Huntelaar credited with scoring the first-ever goal in the Emirates Stadium. The first Arsenal goal netted at the Emirates was scored predictably enough by Thierry Henry. (Gunners fans still hold Gilles Grimandi in eternal esteem for chopping down Edgar Davids as he shaped to score – thus forever denying an ex-Spurs man the chance of striking the first goal in the new ground.)

At a capacity of 60,355, the Emirates is the third biggest stadium in England, after Wembley and Old Trafford. And every one of the crowd assembled on the day of the Villa game sang Arsène Wenger's name in praise of the miracles he had worked for their beloved club – on and off the pitch.

> **Arsenal:** Lehmann, Eboue, Toure, Djourou, Hoyte, Ljungberg, Gilberto, Fabregas, Hleb, Adebayor, Henry. Substitutes: Flamini for Hoyte, Van Persie for Adebayor, Walcott for Ljungberg. Not used: Almunia, Cygan.
> **Aston Villa:** Sorenson, Hughes, Mellberg, Ridgewell, Samuel, Agbonlahor, McGann, Davis, Barry, Angel, Moore. Substitutes: Hendrie for Davis, Djemba-Djemba for Moore, Laursen for Angel. Not used: Taylor, Phillips.
> **Referee:** Graham Poll
> **Attendance:** 60,023

Amy Lawrence wrote after the game in *The Observer*,

> What is the point of a world-class stadium without a world-class team to play in it?'
> So said Arsène Wenger many moons ago, when this arena was nothing more than a set of architect's drawings. It was a pertinent point 73 minutes into this brave new world. Arsenal were trailing, huffing and puffing against a Villa team buoyed by Martin O'Neill's arrival to gatecrash the party. What to do? Enter one Theo Walcott. Now we know. His 17 minute cameo – his first in an Arsenal jersey electrified the pace.

Thus it was Walcott who saved Arsenal's and Wenger's blushes by giving the assist for Gilberto's late equaliser. Walcott disposed, Davis skipped through Villa's backline and crossed for Gilberto to rifle home with an emphatic finish to the joy and relief of the majority present. The Brazilian's 84th-minute leveller made sure the club would not commence life at their shiny new stadium with a defeat as the game ended in a 1-1 stalemate and allowed the Londoners to finish their hugely symbolic opening match with pride intact. As Wenger said of Walcott's injection of pace and urgency, 'His sharpness gave us something we missed.'

Earlier, Aston Villa's captain, the bearded Olof Mellberg, had the honour of scoring the first official goal in the new arena's existence in the 53rd minute. The Gunners would actually have to wait until 23 September 2006 for their first Premiership win at the stadium, when they beat Sheffield United 3-0. Future Arsenal forward Eduardo netted the first European goal at the ground – for Dinamo Zagreb in a Champions League qualifier.

But it was the move to the new ground that took all the headlines. As Wenger looked back on the move later he said,

> The disadvantage was you didn't really feel at home. After coming from Highbury, where you felt so much at home, you think you are playing on a neutral ground. I went into this challenge and I knew that, OK, I had won things with Arsenal, but now we would go into a period that would be more difficult.

To go to a new stadium brought restricted finances at the time and the uncertainty of paying the debt back. The absolute compulsory thing was that we had to stay in the top four. The pressure suddenly became much bigger. I went for this challenge and I must say, thinking back now, it was a massive risk. After some seasons I thanked God that we had managed again to be in the Champions League – but it was only just on a couple of occasions.

The work was really hard and you think that you are not allowed to make any mistake because any point can be costly, which was not so much the case before. These years were – for me certainly as a manager – the most difficult.

When we look back one day, maybe these are not the seasons that will remain most in the memories, but for me this will be the challenge, viewed from a distance, that I'll be the proudest of completing. Because I managed to keep the club at the level that we could survive financially. Now, I think we are on the other side of it and the club can compete again with everyone, financially. Hopefully this will be a period where the club can compete with anybody else again.

35

Slavia Prague (H)

23 October 2007

As European nights go, this match was up there with the best of them in terms of goals and performances. It was also the perfect way for Le Boss to celebrate his fifty-eighth birthday the day before. Wenger, who had joked about the fact no one had bought him any presents, was in relaxed mood, which was helped greatly by the eleven victories on the bounce in the run up to the Champions League game with their Czech visitors from Prague.

When asked what gift he wished for more than anything, the Frenchman replied, 'To play better on Tuesday than they did against Bolton.' Given they eased past their normally truculent guests from Lancashire 2-0 on the previous Saturday, you could have been forgiven for thinking an improvement may not have been forthcoming. The reality was somewhat different.

When asked the day before the Slavia match how he would celebrate his birthday, Wenger replied, 'I do not need any more socks. I may have a glass of wine and watch Newcastle United play Tottenham.' For such a footballing devotee as Wenger, the night must have been an enjoyable one. Especially as Arsenal's bitter North London rivals Spurs succumbed 3-1 at St James' Park. It was to prove to be another good moment during an enjoyable few days – not only for birthday boy Wenger but for the club itself – capped by a near complete performance against the Czechs.

Arsenal: Almunia, Sagna, Toure, Gallas, Clichy, Eboue, Fabregas, Flamini, Hleb, Adebayor, Walcott. Substitutes: Silva for Flamini, Rosicky for Hleb, Bendtner for Adebayor. Not used: Lehmann, Diaby, Diarra, Eduardo.
Slavia Prague: Vaniak, Krajcik, Suchy, Hubacek, Pudil, Senkerik, Svec, Tavares, Kalivoda, Ivana, Vlcek. Substitutes: Belaid for Tavares, Jablonsky for Kalivoda, Volesak for Ivana. Not used: Vorel, Gaucho, Drizd'al, Sourek.
Referee: Stefano Farina (Italy).
Attendance: 59,621

Matt Hughes of *The Times* wrote after the game, 'Arsène Wenger's players responded [to his birthday] by giving him a gift he will treasure … [it was a] majestic performance.'

Wenger's team made the best start possible, with Cesc Fabreagas scoring on five minutes after impressive build-up play by Hleb. The wide-man from Belarus then had a hand in the second, after his shot from a Gael Clichy cross took a significant deflection off the unfortunate Slavia Prague centre-half David Hubacek. An in-form Walcott, still only eighteen years old, fired home number three shortly before half-time, the goal being only his seventh in senior football. The young winger, who had ambitions to play more centrally, showed good composure when 'keeper Vaniak failed to deal with a Daniel Pudil pass back, striking the ball straight at him. With a poise and serenity belying his juvenile bearing, Walcott simply rounded Vaniak before firing the ball into an unguarded net.

The 3-0 scoreline became 4-0 six minutes after half-time, as Hleb deservedly joined the list of goalscorers by slotting home after good approach play from Eboue and Fabregas. Fabregas then created another goal three minutes later by sending Hleb through, who then found Walcott who cut inside before audaciously toe-poking past a bemused and by now bedraggled Vaniak.

The Gunners' sixth was undoubtedly the best of the night, as the team swept forward with pace and precision as they spread the ball the length of the pitch in a matter of seconds, leaving the outclassed Czechs chasing shadows. Hleb ran the ball 30 yards before Walcott moved it on to Fabregas, who slotted home.

As if to prove it was the perfect team performance, substitute Bendtner came on and netted the seventh in the 89th minute, sending the crowd into raptures, the Czechs into despair and Wenger into a birthday wonderland. As David Hytner wrote in his post-match *Guardian* piece, 'The Emirates crowd was in party mood, acclaiming their heroes, including a few from the past – Ian Wright, Patrick Vieira and [the late] David Rocastle. [But] A kid called Theo produced the widest smiles.'

A reflective Arsène Wenger relished the march towards the knockout stages of the Champions League – a twelfth consecutive win in all competitions by a record margin to boot. With the club only two short of their record of fourteen wins from fourteen made twenty seasons ago, he allowed an indulgent nod towards one of his young English signings in the aftermath of the victory against the hapless Czechs.

Wenger said in a rare outburst of lavish praise,

There was a touch of Thierry Henry about Walcott's second goal. The first quality is to be composed and not to rush things. Once Theo scored his first, you saw him much more. When they opened up the space, you could see his runs and pace, and the fact he is clinical in front of goal.

Walcott was thrust into the limelight as a callow seventeen-year-old by a muddled Sven-Göran Erikson who picked him for his England squad for the 2006 World Cup in Germany – and then failed to pick him during the tournament itself. Wenger further commented,

You complain in England that you don't have many strikers. Theo is one of them. He has all the ingredients to be a top striker; fantastic pace, intelligence and his technique is improving. You complain you don't have many strikers and accuse Arsenal of not producing enough England players – Theo is one of them. He is intelligent, has fantastic pace and his technique is improving. Theo has the talent, that is why he is at Arsenal. I'm convinced he has the talent and I'm convinced he has the ingredients in him. Two months ago I was 'crazy' not to buy players and we were not even rated in England's top seven.

Walcott is clinical in front of goal, he did not panic with the first one and with the second there was a really clinical finish. The problem is not to hurry too much, you need to be patient. But we've seen some great performances and everyone is still improving and there is more to come from this team.

Walcott himself said, 'People will say that my second goal was like a Thierry Henry finish and I watched him in training all the time. I had a chance tonight and I took it. It was an absolutely brilliant team performance.'

The margin of Arsenal's victory also equalled the biggest win in the Champions League, matching Juventus' 2003 7-0 demolition of Olympiakos.

As birthday boy, Wenger concluded,

> We wanted three points and to play well but you can't predict that. Everything went for us. We scored the first goal with the first chance. I wanted Theo to start in a big game and he played well. He is calm and clinical in front of goal.

It was that kind of night for Walcott. It was that kind of week for Wenger.

36

AC Milan (A)
4 March 2008

Arsenal's Champions League last sixteen second-leg against AC Milan at the San Siro was played less than two weeks after Eduardo's lower limb was shattered by Birmingham's Mark Taylor, in a 2-2 draw that was to have severe repercussions for the team for the rest of the season. But not in Milan. The goalless first leg rendered the match open, if slanted favourably towards the Italians.

Mindful of brutal tackling, Wenger was asked by the Italian press whether he would send out any of his players to intentionally hurt an opposing player. His principled answer was a direct retort to the traumatic events of St Andrews:

No chance, no chance if you kick the great players out of games then why should people watch football? Great players make football a bit special – an art. If you kick them it is not acceptable. In Italy, what do the teams do when they play against Milan? Take Kaka, get him out of the game. And you know how they will deal with that. But we will be faithful to what we do, we will try to deal with him by cutting the connections to him. We will play zonal and will not mark him man-to-man.

It was a brave move given Milan's exemplary record in Europe. Given no team had retained the Champions League since it moved from being the European Cup, the Rossoneri's three finals appearances in only five years represented at the time the most dominant era by a single team.

Wenger added defiantly the day before,

I do not like to go away from home thinking my team just has to defend. With a 0-0 result, we know that we have to attack as well as defend.

From the first game, we have the belief we can beat them because we dominated the game – that always has an impact on the second game.

We will need patience against them in Milan but our pace can be a good asset as well.

Milan have shown in Europe that they can deal with all sorts of opposition, they can slow the game down. What Milan do well is put you to their pace, and when Kaka gets the ball they can have sudden acceleration which can kill you.

We will have to adapt to that because we like to play always at a high pace. In the end we should have won the first game because we were able to keep the game at a consistent high pace. We like to play at a consistent high pace, they like to play slow-quick.

As he added prophetically, 'The first leg 0-0 is not a bad result because you know defence is not good enough. You know will have to attack as well.'

Referring to his team's stunning 5-1 in the same stadium, albeit against Milan's city rivals Inter, he said,

> The 5-1 is a big inspiration – we came here in a desperate situation and had to make a big score – and we made it. I believe we are highly focused again for this game and the team spirit is very high. We are confident and up for it.

They certainly were as his young side secured a result that was labelled as good as any in the club's growing collection of memorable European matches.

AC Milan: Kalac, Maldini, Nesta, Oddo, Kaladze, Pirlo, Kaka, Ambrosini, Gattuso, Alexandre Pato, Inzaghi. Substitutes: Gilardino for Inzaghi. Not used: Fiori, Bonera, Favalli, Simic, Emerson, Gourcuff.
Arsenal: Almunia, Senderos, Clichy, Gallas, Sagna, Diaby, Eboue, Fabregas, Flamini, Hleb, Adebayor. Substitutes: Walcott for Eboue, Silva for Hleb. Not used: Lehmann, Hoyte, Denilson, van Persie, Bendtner.
Referee: Konrad Plautz
Attendance: 81,879

Make no mistake, this was a vintage Milan side, even if they were starting to show their age. The Champions League holders fielded the evergreen one-club man Maldini, defensive lynchpin Nesta, Kaka – who needed no introduction – the commanding Gattuso, promising young Brazilian Pato, the powerful Inzaghi and the wily Pirlo with his immaculate technique. To win 2-0 in front of a sell-out crowd ensured the Gunners fully deserved the standing ovation they gained from the fair-minded Italian fans after the referee's final whistle.

This was a performance of resolve, grit and fortitude – with no little skill and attacking intent thrown in. Mathieu Flamini and Cesc Fabregas in the heat of the midfield battle had the game of their lives completely eclipsing the household opposition names. It may have explained the space they allowed the Spaniard with only six minutes remaining in a tense tie. With Cesc 25 yards out from goal, he let fly with a powerfully low shot that entered the net. It was a moment to savour as he and his teammates – along with the vociferous 6,000 travelling Arsenal fans located high up in the stands above – celebrated wildly. Fabregas eventually slid onto his knees near Wenger's dug-out in an eruption of joy.

With AC Milan knowing the game was up, Adebayor netted number two in the 89th minute to clinch a memorable 2-0 win, which seasoned Arsenal watchers rated as better than the 5-1 win over Inter at the same stadium five years previously. Once again, Wenger's men merited their triumph at the Stadio Meazza. The result also signified Milan's first home defeat to an English side. As Wenger said afterwards,

> I have big respect for Milan, but my team deserves a lot of credit – having come here and beaten a team like them. We have given the performance we wanted. We played with organisation and never dropped off. We did not give them time and went forward every time we could. We played with authority, maturity, talent and intelligence.

We have knocked out the holders. This team is very young, but we have won at Bernabeu and San Siro, so you need some quality to do that. On the day we were better than Milan, but maybe we play against them on Friday and it will be different.

I feel tonight the players deserve a lot of credit, because our confidence level in the camp has dropped a bit. We have not been in the most positive environment recently, from the media. I like the fact the team finds the mental strength to play without restriction.

Now we have to keep a good balance between belief and humility – that is a very important quality as well because it allows a team to be consistent.

The growing process of a team is a bit like a wave, it goes up suddenly, then down with a few bad results, then it goes up high again.

This result would live long in the memory. Unfortunately, Wenger was proved correct about the team's fragile confidence, which rode high after this game, only to be brought back down to earth with a juddering thump in the quarter-finals against Liverpool. But for Wenger's class of 2008, they would always have Milan.

37

Liverpool (A)

8 April 2008

Early April 2008 saw a Liverpool trilogy destined to play a large part in shaping the Gunners, season. Unfortunately, it did not end positively. In the Champions League quarter-final first leg against the Reds at Emirates, which ended 1-1 (Adebayor), Arsène Wenger was furious at the Dutch referee Pieter Vink. He certainly appeared to have a strong case for his rage after Alexander Hleb appeared to have been impeded by a tug from Netherlands forward Dirk Kuyt.

The Frenchman stormed afterwards,

> It was a blatant penalty, under the eyes of the referee. I feel we were not rewarded for what we produced – and we had the chances to win it. We were a bit unlucky with a big decision of the referee on the penalty. It's difficult to take, but we have to swallow it even if it is difficult to understand how we did not win the game, because we had a lot of possession and a lot of chances. Liverpool created very little, and the whole second half was played in one half. If you look at our amount of possession compared to Liverpool, it is frightening that we could only come out of it with a 1-1. I cannot fault the players. We were unlucky in the circumstances. The game was played in one half in the second period and it was difficult because Liverpool defended well.

The scene was set for the dramatic second leg, but before that the pair of English giants had to face each other in a League match in North London with Wenger noting, 'It is now a little bit of a survival battle – the one who is still good after three games is the one who is the better team.'

In the League game, Pepe Reina sent a 70-yard ball to Torres, who played a one-two with Yossi Benayoun before striking a low shot into the corner. Arsenal lost their shape and played without rhythm in an attempt to claw their way back into the game. The tactic was to work in part as Bendtner nodded in a Cesc Fabregas dead ball. But it was two points dropped in what was to be an ultimately futile chase for the title. Wenger said afterwards, ahead of the biggest match in Arsenal's season, 'The second leg will be a test for us – but we have the desire to do it.'

Not for the first time, his faith in his players around this period did not match the final outcome.

Liverpool: Reina, Carragher, Skrtel, Hyypia, Aurelio, Gerrard, Alonso, Mascherano, Kuyt, Torres, Crouch. Substitutes: Babel for Crouch, Riise for Torres, Arbeloa for Kuyt. Not used: Itandje, Voronin, Benayoun, Lucas.

Arsenal: Almunia, Toure, Gallas, Senderos, Clichy, Eboue, Flamini, Fabregas, Diaby, Hleb, Adebayor. Substitutes: Silva for Flamini, Walcott for Eboue, Van Persie for Diaby. Not used: Lehmann, Song Billong, Bendtner, Justin Hoyte.
Referee: Peter Frojdfeldt (Sweden).
Attendance: 41,985

Kevin McCarra of *The Guardian* wrote in wonder,

> This match leaves everyone who gawped at the wonder of it in the grip of their memories. Recriminations, too, ought to be put on hold although Arsenal, easing ahead on the away goals rule after tying the score here at 2-2 in the 84th minute, will be aghast over a loss inflicted primarily by Steven Gerrard's penalty moments later [but] only those with a partisan interest can dwell on that when there was so much to revel in over the course of a contest that must rank high in the entire history of this tournament.

This was a gripping game played out in front of a raucous Anfield atmosphere playing host to another passionate European night. Both teams played as if their seasons were on the line, which they were. Arsenal, so lethargic in the previous game against the Merseysiders, if not the first leg, started the game with a point to prove. Abou Diaby, beefing up the midfield, burst through after Hleb fed him a ball to use his considerable power to run on to fired a low shot, which Reina couldn't prevent entering the net. Yet Hyppia's equaliser on the half-hour mark galvanised the home team after the Gunners threatened further. On 69 minutes, Torres spun and shot in one movement, netting a goal in front of the Kop to make it 2-1.

Yet Arsenal did lie not down, and the introduction of Theo Walcott energised the Londoners. This game could have been a defining moment in the young winger's career. As it was, his mazy, dazzling, speedy 80-yard burst that left Liverpool defenders trailing in his wake proved to be a small footnote in his development. It was a shame, as the way the youngster fearlessly ran at the home defence was as mesmerising as it was gripping to watch as he drove deep in the opposition's box before unselfishly squaring to Adebayor, who couldn't miss from yards out to make it 2-2 on the night. If the score stayed the same, Arsenal were through to the semi-finals of the Champions League. Some fans from London were still celebrating the goal when Liverpool, straight from kick-off won a penalty through Babel – although many Gooners still assert that Kolo Toure's challenge, clumsy as it was, did not merit a penalty. Arsenal fans at the away end were soon stung from their reveries as Gerrard fired into the top corner to break their hearts with only four minutes left on the watch. Still Arsenal poured forward, only to be caught by Babel's late goal and Liverpool's fourth to make it 4-2. The last goal was irrelevant and soon forgotten – unlike Arsenal's cruel, late exit.

Afterwards Wenger was furious and blamed poor refereeing for his side's elimination. He said,

> Over the two games we were the better team. This defeat is hard to swallow. I felt the game was over at 2-2. Then there was a dodgy penalty and we started to lose concentration. Over the two games this is hard to swallow. The big decisions over penalties have gone

against us. It is difficult to take, the players in the dressing room are very down because they believe week after week the decisions are going against them.

He asserted,

It was not a penalty. I have seen the replay but we were denied a clear penalty last week. That was a real penalty, this one wasn't. At 2-2 we had a great chance to kill the game off but we lacked experience and made big mistakes.

But we still feel a great sense of injustice – we were three minutes from qualifying.

Liverpool manager Rafa Benitez told the *Daily Express*, 'This will go down as another great European night.'

Another great night for the Anfield club – not for Arsenal as once again Wenger and his team were left to rue on what might have been.

38

Sheffield United (H)

23 September 2008

This match was arguably the apogee of Arsène Wenger's experiment with youth. It was a fascination that turned into an obsession, which started as a necessity, with the club being forced to save money in preparation for the move from Highbury.

The night was a glorious tribute to Wenger's total and utter belief in youngsters. The Gunners' youthful team, with an average age of just nineteen, gave Championship side Sheffield United's first team a footballing lesson that was as tremendous to watch as it must have been embarrassing to view as a Blades fan.

The talk beforehand was of rising star Jack Wilshere, aged sixteen years 267 days, starting his first competitive game for the club. But he wasn't even to be the youngest Arsenal player in the squad for the Sheffield United game; first-year scholar Emmanuel Frimpong had that distinction, at nine days younger than Wilshere.

Wenger said proudly ahead of the game,

There is a possibility it will be the youngest side ever. In the first team there are many players around 20. In the Carling Cup we will keep a few in there but the side will be more between 16 and 19. At Arsenal you can say 20 and 21-year-olds are the experienced players.

You are likely to see Gavin Hoyte, Abu Ogogu, Aaron Ramsey, Mark Randall, Jack Wilshere, Fran Merida and Carlos Vela. Maybe Bendtner will play. Song, Djourou and Lukasz Fabianski will be the experienced players. But you will have players like Emmanuel Frimpong and Jay Emmanuel-Thomas so it will be a very young side.

But it was a very good side too. Far too good for poor Sheffield United, including the much lamented Gary Speed.

Arsenal: Fabianski, Hoyte, Djourou, Song, Gibbs, Randall, Ramsey, Merida, Wilshere, Bendtner, Vela. Substitutes: Lansbury for Song, Coquelin for Merida, Simpson for Bendtner. Not used: Mannone, Emmanuel-Thomas, Ogogo, Frimpong.
Sheffield United: Kenny, Halford, Morgan, Kilgallon, Naysmith, Cotterill, Speed, Quinn, Montgomery, Beattie, Webber. Substitutes: Maughton for Cotterill, Hendrie for Speed, Robertson for Beattie. Not used: Bennett, Sharp, Geary, Ehiogu.
Referee: Phil Dowd
Attendance: 56,632

Nicklas Bendtner commenced the thrashing in this League Cup third-round tie on 30 minutes with a strike from 20 yards before netting again shortly after from close range. Cancun born Carlos Vela – of whom Wenger said was 'so cool he made him smile' – curled in a brilliant third ahead of the break. The nineteen-year-old striker made it 4-0 on 50 minutes with a ludicrous scoop over the visitors' vastly experienced 'keeper Paddy Kenny – who still couldn't do a thing to save it, such was his shock at the audacity of the young Mexican. The striker completed his hat-trick with three minutes remaining to make it a half dozen, and send their thoroughly outclassed Yorkshire travellers home despondent.

But it was fledgling starlet, Stevenage-born but Hitchin-reared Jack Wilshere, a tender sixteen, that had home fans drooling more than anyone, firing home a fifth goal. In doing so, he broke long-standing records, becoming not only the youngest-ever player to start a competitive first team game for the Arsenal, but also as the club's youngest-ever goalscorer.

This game and Jack's goal proved that home fans – who had to endure ignorant jibes from fans (and certain managers) up and down the country at their lack of English players – now had two very real young English prospects to laud. No wonder Arsenal fans were genuinely excited after this game. Wenger was too:

> I would say yes these are the best crop of young players I have had. Because there is not one player who has not the real quality of the Premier League in any position. The biggest challenge is for the club to keep them all together and slowly integrate them into the first team. Many of them already play there: Djourou, Song, Bendtner, Fabianski play already, Vela too. I think that's why when you're under immense pressure to buy in every transfer window when you know you have these players behind already, [it] nearly kills you, the work we have done.

Yet it was Jack Wilshere that everyone wanted to hear the Frenchman speak about. They weren't to be disappointed.

> He was 15 when he first impressed me. He's 16 now and last year a few times I integrated him in our first team training sessions. He didn't look at all out of place. Straight away football was natural for him.
>
> He is a quiet boy, very determined, very focused. The talent is there you have seen that again tonight. It is always difficult when you are the manager of a boy with talent like that, you are always a little bit cautious to put too much pressure on him and too high a level of expectation. I believe it is all in there and that I have the responsibilities to nurture him and to get him at the right moment and the right development in the next two or three years. The ages of 16 to 19 are very important for the development of a football player. At the moment he has skipped a few classes.
>
> People tell me he is a little bit like Liam Brady because he has good balance and change of direction. I believe later Jack Wilshere he will be a central midfielder or behind the strikers.

Wenger also talked in glowing terms of rising left back Kieran Gibbs noting with conviction,

> I play him now at left back because I feel he can be very good there. He has a tremendous engine, good technique and he's a very reliable boy. I am convinced that with the way we

play football he can be a great left-back. I wouldn't be scared to play any individual of this 11 in the Premier League, altogether I don't know, but all the individual players who played tonight have the talent, for example Kieran Gibbs. He is a very young left-back.

I believe that the team played football the way we want to play. We showed a good mixture of individual talent, maturity and collective spirit. The team remained focused on the kind of football we wanted to play and respected that, it was very pleasing.

I believe everyone in his position has done very well. From goalkeeper Fabianski up to Bendtner and Vela they were great. You know already Bendtner and you discovered maybe a bit more about Vela. He is a clinical finisher. I am pleased as well with our midfield, and our defence was serious and stayed strong – we looked like the complete team and I'm very happy and proud of that.

I'm not as surprised as you because I see them every day but you never know how they'll respond on the big stage. They just went out there are played with the belief we want them to have and with the spirit we want them to have.

You let them play how they played tonight and suddenly you say 'sorry you don't play anymore'. For me that is not serious, no matter how far we go we have to stick to our policy. These players do not play like kids, they play like people with intelligence, with talent and with spirit.

Carlos Vela I think he's a player who has everything in his locker of a good striker. He's agile, good first touch, very calm in front of goal, clinical and quick finisher and I just think he's top class.

39

Barcelona (A)

6 April 2010

Arsène Wenger saw his side outplayed, outpassed and outclassed for much of their home leg quarter-final Champions League tie against Catalan giants Barcelona. Yet they still managed to finish the match level after a late Fabregas penalty – taken with what turned out to be a broken leg – saw them fight back from 2-0 down to draw 2-2. An Ibrahimovic-inspired Barca presented the Gunners with huge problems to solve, but the North Londoners had their moments and the European champions looking rattled at times. This, in turn, gave Wenger hope for the second leg in the imposing Nou Camp.

'I think it is more balanced than the impression people have,' Wenger said in Catalonia the day before the tie.

> If you look at the first game again, we analysed it very well. Many times they gave us big problems in the first part of the game but if you look at the number of chances we created through the whole game it is quite interesting.
>
> But I believe there is no room for patience now. You score goals tomorrow night when you can but you need a big discipline, a big organisation for a big part in the game. It is for sure if it is still 0-0 in the last part of the game we can throw everything at them but we have to try to be very well disciplined and not to hide when we have the ball.

Wenger said,

> The players have come back from the dead once and can do it again.
>
> They know they escaped being out of the competition and we have a chance we have to take tomorrow. It's Easter you know, a time of resurrection. That's what we want to do tomorrow night.
>
> The late come-backs this season show that this team has character. We've shown that consistently throughout the season. In the Champions League it's the same. People have written us off, but we're halfway through and will give a good game to Barcelona.

Loyal as ever to his team whatever the odds Wenger added, 'This team has character, and when you have character you always have hope. We have character and quality. With character and quality you can fight anywhere in the world.'

But not every team in the world boasted Lionel Messi.

Arsenal: Almunia, Sagna, Vermaelen, Silvestre, Clichy, Denilson, Diaby, Nasri, Rosicky, Walcott, Bendtner. Substitutes: Eboue for Silvestre, Eduardo for Rosicky. Not used: Fabianski, Campbell, Traore, Eastmond, Merida.

FC Barcelona: Valdes, Dani Alves, Marquez, Milito, Abidal, Busquets, Xavi, Keita, Messi, Bojan, Pedro. Substitutes: Maxwell for Bojan, Yaya Toure for Abidal. Not used: Pinto, Iniesta, Fontas, Henry, Jeffren.

Referee: Wolfgang Stark (Germany)

Attendance: 95,486

Arsenal and their estimated 7,000 travelling fans dared to dream for three minutes in the Nou Camp – the time between Nicklas Bendtner's unlikely breakaway goal on 18 minutes and Lionel Messi's equaliser 180 seconds later. Messi then fired home in the 37th minute before audaciously chipping Alumunia just before half-time to seal the tie. In truth, a depleted Gunners side did well to keep the goals conceded to three before Messi hit his fourth on 87 minutes to seal the tie 4-1 and 6-3 on aggregate.

As Oliver Kay wrote in *The Times* the next morning,

> All season long Arsène Wenger has talked of elevating football to an art form and, so, whatever the depth of his disappointment last night, the aesthete inside the Arsenal manager cannot have failed to be moved a masterclass from the incomparable Lionel Messi … witnessed in succession, they were testament to his myriad strengths – mesmerising footwork and close control, lovely balance, beautiful improvisation and, for someone who lacks physical stature, remarkable degrees of power and persistence.

Kay's colleague Rob Hughes added, 'Lionel Messi produced a finishing masterclass to kill off Arsenal's Champions League hopes and leave the watching world breathless with admiration.'

Wenger was certainly included in that list as he spoke magnamously after the game:

> First I want to congratulate Barcelona and wish them good luck. Over the two games they deserved to qualify. They are a very good side but of course they have Messi who can make a difference at any moment in the game. He can take advantage of every mistake we make.
>
> I believe we played quite well. We started strong, had a good opportunity to score the second goal and were a bit unlucky because we had a good chance when Bendtner was not offside. The regret I have is that we made too many mistakes defensively for a game like that. They were always first on the ball and we were punished for it.
>
> I believe Barcelona are the best side at the moment in Europe. It is a cup and if we had taken every opportunity tonight we could have made life very difficult for them.
>
> I feel before they equalised we had a great chance to score the second goal but we made a bad decision with the final ball. Had we scored then the doubt would have been serious. They came back straight after that to 1-1.
>
> If you look at the age of our team we were very, very young today. What we have done is very positive because we had six or seven players under 23 in the team and we had plenty of opportunities. Where we have shown that we lack maturity is in the final ball.
>
> The defeat is very difficult to handle because when you go out of the Champions League the next day you are in front of a very empty future. We have to deal with the

disappointment and make sure that we are ready for the next game. I congratulated Pep Guardiola after the match and wished him well for the rest of the competition.

Barcelona is more than Messi. They have other players in the team who are top class. They are an exceptional team with an exceptional player and in the exceptional games the exceptional players make the difference.

Tonight we missed seven or eight players but I don't think we gave them too much respect tonight. We started well, we won some good possession from Barcelona and we dominated through some spells in the game. They are a good side. In the first game, yes we respected them too much but I don't think we did tonight.

Lionel Messi is very young but he can achieve a lot. For example I don't know how many players in the world who could score that fourth goal he scored. It looks impossible but he makes it possible. He has something exceptional and he is in his prime. This boy now has six or seven years in front of him and if nothing happens to him he can reach unbelievable levels.

Although disappointed, at least those Arsenal fans present on such a wondrous Nou Camp night could tell their grandchildren they saw Lionel Messi play against their team at the peak of his career.

The Gunners certainly didn't hide, but when faced with the world's best player in Lionel Messi they didn't win either. Then again not many teams did against the Barca of Pep Guardiola.

40

Newcastle United (A)

5 February 2011

The game took place the week Newcastle United sold Andy Carroll to Liverpool for a staggering £35 million.

In what were to be prophetic words Wenger added, 'We expect Newcastle to be up for it against us and so we prepare ourselves to meet a good team.'

Yet Arsène Wenger was confident his team were finally showing consistency during the first half of the 2010/11 season. Speaking before the game in Newcastle, at which point Arsenal stood only five points off leaders Manchester United, he explained,

> For me it is down to our performances and our consistency because we have quality and talent that nobody denies. But also we have spirit, attitude and a great togetherness. You can see that when we play. There is something special in our team that is coming out from game to game. That's why I firmly believe in our chance.

This game would see his belief – and the belief of the 3,000 travelling fans as well as millions of Gooners worldwide – suffer an almighty blow. A blow that would arguably affect them psychologically for the rest of the season as accusations over their so-called soft underbelly resurfaced with a vengeance.

Newcastle United: Harper, Coloccini, Jose Enrique, Williamson, Simpson, Nolan, Barton, Gutierrez, Tiote, Lovenkrands, Best. Substitutes: Ranger for Lovenkrands, Guthrie for Best. Not used: Krul, Campbell, Perch, Shane Ferguson, Richardson.
Arsenal: Szczesny, Sagna, Koscielny, Djourou, Clichy, Diaby, Fabregas, Walcott, Wilshere, Arshavin, Van Persie. Substitutes: Squillaci for Djourou, Rosicky for Arshavin, Eboue for Walcott. Not used: Almunia, Gibbs, Chamakh, Bendtner.
Referee: Phil Dowd
Attendance: 51,561

This was the game above all others non-Arsenal fans chose to illustrate their perception that the club was lacking in mental strength. As the Gunners raced into a 4-0 lead in just 26 minutes, any away fans who had missed the opening salvo as they sampled the delights of the city's many lively pre-match hostelries may have consoled themselves with the fact there were to be more visitors' goals to follow. Yet even if there were not to be any further strikes, they may have felt safe in the knowledge that three important points were to be heading back to London with the minimum of fuss.

Unfortunately for them, Arsène Wenger, his team and Arsenal fans everywhere were to receive the shock of their lives.

A goal down in only 42 seconds from Theo Walcott, owner Mike Ashley had barely taken his seat when the Magpies found themselves 2-0 down on three minutes, with Johan Djourou's first goal for the North Londoners. It was to prove the high point of his match as he was substituted a few minutes into the second half with a knee injury, only to be replaced by the hapless Sebastian Squillaci who would feature in many of Wenger's 'Worst Buy' elevens. His second half performance would see to that.

However, Wenger's men were still to make it 3-0 after Djourou's maiden goal when Van Persie notched a third with only ten minutes showing on the clock. When the Dutchman netted the fourth on 26 minutes, many Newcastle supporters were seen heading for the exits – or at the very least an early half-time beer.

As the half-time boos rained down on the home team, Arsenal fans were joyously celebrating an extraordinary first half – with little expectation that the second period would be even more climactic.

Paul Hayward writing in the *Observer* newspaper the next morning reported dryly, 'The only way Newcastle could have found a use for their £35 million windfall at this stage was to pile it up in banknotes between their posts to stem the tide of Arsenal goals.'

Newcastle's comeback was as unforeseen as it was shattering to Arsenal. The moment the tide turned could be traced to Abou Diaby, so influential in midfield in the opening 45 minutes, disastrously losing his cool, as it turned out after a brutal Joey Barton challenge that was less a tackle and more a desperate attempt at provocation. It worked. Diaby was sent off after grabbing the incendiary Barton by the back of the neck, and Newcastle's unlikely revival had begun.

A few moments later, an unconvincing challenge by Laurent Koscielny on Leon Best brought the first goal via a Barton penalty. Best then netted number two. As Newcastle, urged on by an increasingly loud home support, carried on attacking, Arsenal conceded another penalty with agent provocateur Barton scoring again.

Holding on for those frenetic last eight minutes proved a bridge too far for Arsenal, as a soft Clichy clearance fell to powerhouse Cheik Tiote, who struck the ball perfectly from 25 yards to score the goal of his life – rendering the scoreline a ridiculously improbable 4-4. In doing so, he brought the house down, indelibly shattering Arsenal hearts in the process.

A crushed Wenger said afterwards,

It's very frustrating because we played a good game and we had an opportunity to take three points in the title race. Newcastle kept fighting, I knew at 4-0 the game was not over because it was important to keep our nerves and continue to play. A team that has already lost the game, when they get back into the game you are always under threat. That was very important for us, not to allow them to get back into the game. Therefore, we are certainly guilty tonight by going down to ten men. Certainly, more psychologically than on the footballing side. We were worried too much on protecting our lead after that because we were down to ten men. Instead of continuing to play, we invited pressure. Afterwards we were very unlucky with some decisions as well. I cannot do anything about that.

It was a completely unnecessary sending off and I believe Barton was very lucky to stay on the pitch because of his tackle on Diaby. Diaby is very disappointed at the moment, it's better not to talk to him. He has to try to get over that. It's a shame because he had a great first half. He had an outstanding game. His reaction could be explained a little bit by the fact that he has been injured so many times [from] bad tackles that he lost a little bit quickly his nerves. This boy has been out for a long time and many times. Certainly the tackler provoked his reaction.

I was surprised by both penalty decisions. But I am not the referee and I don't think my opinion is very important now because we cannot come back and change it.

As Wenger added portentously, 'Mathematically the damage is two points, psychologically the damage is bigger tonight because everyone is very disappointed in the dressing room. Only the future will tell.'

With the League Cup final at Wembley against huge underdogs Birmingham City fast approaching, no one was more acutely aware of the harm this destructive draw would be to Arsenal than Wenger himself.

41

Barcelona (H)

16 February 2011

Henry Winter's match report in the *Telegraph* summed up the night:

> Lightning rarely strikes once against Barcelona. Here it struck twice. One-nil down to the best team on the planet, struggling to see the ball, let alone the goal, Arsenal responded in sensational style, scoring twice in five minutes late on. This was a turnaround born of resilience, a victory rooted in character. Arsène Wenger made some tactical tweaks, setting Barcelona new tests with the introduction of Andrei Arshavin and Nicklas Bendtner, but what happened between the 78th and 83rd minutes stemmed from a simple refusal to surrender.

Kevin McCarra of *The Guardian* wrote,

> Arsène Wenger can settle for feeling proud of the maturity of Arsenal players whose temperaments did not shrivel even when Barcelona were at their most intimidatingly fluent ... Meeting Barcelona is a predicament for virtually all teams but Arsenal's case is unusual. Rather than being the normal contrast of styles, this encounter saw Guardiola's side taking on opponents who would like nothing better than to emulate their methods – Arsenal withstood that comparison.

Arsenal were unwavering in their resolution to avoid another chastening first half experience in North London at the hands of the world's best team. With memories still fresh from being passed off the pitch in the opening 45 minutes by Messi and Co. the previous season before bravely fighting back to draw 2-2, Arsenal stood toe to toe with the Catalan giants this time around.

Wenger's team resolve was to produce a night never to be forgotten.

Arsenal: Szczesny, Eboue, Clichy, Djourou, Koscielny, Song, Wilshere, Walcott, Nasri, Fabregas, Van Persie. Substitutes: Arshavin for Song, Bendtner for Walcott. Not used: Almunia, Rosicky, Denilson, Squillaci, Gibbs.
Barcelona: Valdes, Dani Alves, Pique, Xavi, Villa, Messi, Busquets, Pedro, Maxwell, Abidal, Iniesta. Substitutes: Keita for Villa, Adriano for Iniesta. Not used: Pinto, Bojan, Mascherano, Milito, Afellay.
Referee: Nicola Rizzoli (Italy)
Attendance: 59,927

Wenger's men started more impressively, with Barca laden with a certain complacency stemming from their games in 2010. Born a whisker from the city of Barcelona and tempted away from under their noses, Cesc Fabregas showed his innate invention by lifting the ball over the heads of the Catalans' defence for van Persie to run on to, but their goalkeeper Victor Valdes was equal to the task and performed a vital block to deny van Persie.

Soon the visitors were into their stride and producing exquisite tiki-taka shapes, which was the copyright of all Guardiola's teams. David Villa fed Messi, but the Argentinian maestro was guilty of rare over-elaboration, sending his finish over Gunners custodian Wojciech Szczesny – but thankfully for Arsenal fans generating a raucous atmosphere – wide of the post. The collective intake of breath was audible. It was the clearest indication that Barca were finding their rhythm after being swamped by the force of Arsenal's impressive start.

Andres Iniesta nearly played Villa through on, and moments later Messi was uncharacteristically profligate as he spurned a second chance, this time chipping weakly into Szczesny hands even though he had far more time and space than he usually did to fashion a goal from.

Wenger's men refused to be cowed, as they were the season before, and it required a headed clearance from a Fabregas cross by the Frenchman Eric Abidal as Van Persie lurked to ease mounting pressure from the home side. But, just when Gunners fans could be forgiven for thinking they were on top, Barcelona shattered the illusion.

On 26 minutes, Messi (who else) created a goal from nothing, with a perfectly weighted ball that sliced through Arsenal's defensive rear guard, allowing the prolific Villa to drive on and finish with his usual precision. Szczesny then did well to hinder Pedro at the near post, even if a few minutes later Dutchman Van Persie should have shown far more awareness in shooting high and wide when he found himself in a good position.

The Flea, Messi's nickname, moved the ball into the net on half-time, but was correctly judged offside before the whistle was blown on a breathless first half. It was a first half that showed how far the club had come in a year when playing the world's best team.

After the interval, both teams started at the same momentum as before. The visitors complained loudly that a penalty should have been given after Villa engineered a collision with Laurent Koscielny, before Van Persie tested Valdes with a rasping shot from the edge of the area.

It was proving not to be Messi's night in front of goal. On 67 minutes, he should have doubled his team's lead but fired into the side netting with a chance he would normally score from.

But Wenger's team kept their nerve and their discipline in the face of constant Barcelona pressure, and extended spells of possession. They received their reward for such persistence in the 78th minute. Van Persie fired a low shot from a tight angle, confounded a lethargic Valdes, beating him at his near post to the unrestrained joy around in the stands and on the pitch.

Like a prize fighter wobbling to the underdog after a sucker punch, Barcelona desperately tried to cling on to what they had. The Emirates crowd, so long derided by people jealous of the shiny new stadium with the poor acoustics, roared their backing, turning the atmosphere into what many seasoned Arsenal watchers described as the best they had experienced since the move from Highbury.

The team and the fans got their reward for such devotion and tenacity only five minutes later, when Andre Arshavin – four goals at Anfield aside – gave his best moment in an Arsenal shirt back running on to the end of Nasri's cross from the right-hand side to guide an exact finish past a clearly stunned Valdes. Cue pandemonium. And seven minutes later, cue an amazing victory over the world's most successful not to mention best footballing side.

A pleased Wenger said after the game,

It was unusual for us to go into a home game as the underdogs, but it took a bit of the pressure off. But we had a huge desire to win and viewed it as a good opportunity to show we were a different team to the previous year [when they lost 6-3 on aggregate].

I accepted that Barcelona would have more of the ball than us – sometimes it's best to put yourself in the frame of mind knowing it is possible because then you are prepared to deal with it. If you are not prepared mentally it can shock you and take your confidence away.

At half-time I told them it was important to keep their belief and push more on certain players because we gave them a bit too much room in the first half. I felt we could change the game, we had to remember the previous season when we came back in the last 20 minutes.

Wenger continued,

We stuck to what we wanted to do, and that – as well as our mental strength and togetherness – was dominant to our success. Nobody showed any sign of dropping their focus. It was a massive night because everything clicked. Our fans were fantastic – like the players, they refused to give in. It was a night to show the whole world how fantastic football can be.

I am highly delighted because it was a special football match. The game promised a lot and absolutely fulfilled the promises between two exceptional football teams who always try to play. We were not only strong on the physical side but on the mental side, we kept resilient. We took advantage of one special piece of skill from Van Persie and the goal for the second was after some good build-up play. It was a special night. When we suffered, the fans were still very positive.

I am proud for Arsenal FC. Everyone urged us to play differently to our nature so it is good. I believe that it can strengthen the belief in our philosophy.

A philosophy that succeeded in beating the best team in the world.

42

Birmingham City (N)

27 February 2011

Bendtner and an own goal saw Arsenal knockout Wigan Athletic in the quarter-finals after a comprehensive 4-0 victory on Tyneside in round four, the goals coming from Bendtner, Walcott (2) and an own goal. Spurs were annihilated 4-1 on a memorable night at White Hart Lane in round three. The goals coming from Nasri (2), Arshavin and Henri Lansbury in front of 5,000 joyous travelling Gooners, who serenaded the Spurs fans with a round of 'Shall we make a DVD?' – a reference to the perception the White Hart Lane outfit were far too ready to commit their somewhat rare victories against Arsenal to commemorative DVDs.

Arsenal had qualified for the final after a two legged semi-final victory against Ipswich Town, 3-1 on aggregate. The shock of the 1-0 defeat at Portman Road following an insipid performance, was brushed off with a 3-0 at the Emirates against the Tractor Boys, with Fabregas, Bendtner and Koscielny netting to send the Gunners through to Wembley.

Arsène Wenger, speaking ahead of the League final, said he would not be satisfied if the club only won the Carling Cup because he wanted so much more from the season.

Musing about winning a trophy for the first time since May 2005 ahead of the Wembley showpiece, he said,

For me to be satisfied I must feel that the team must go as far as it can. Why should we limit our ambition at the end of February? We don't want to win this trophy and then consider the season over. The real quality of the players and me is to go as far as we can. If we don't win the Carling Cup we will continue for the rest. That time has come for us. I think so because we are close in every competition to have a chance of winning and this Cup is the closest one. You reassure yourself when you know you can do things.

On the risk of freezing on the day of the final Wenger said,

There is always a risk but you fight very hard to be in this kind of position. In football, when you lose you have to accept defeat. But what is important when you go into a Final is that you give absolutely everything. You do not want to go into a Final with fear that if you lose it will be dramatic. What you want is to go into the final and give everything to win it and that is how we approach the game. No matter what happens we have such a big end of season in front of us, whether we win or don't win. What is the most important is that we have promised ourselves to give absolutely everything in every game until the end of the season and that is the target we have in front of us.

They were to prove prophetic words ahead of the drama that lay in store.

Arsenal: Szczesny, Sagna, Koscielny, Djourou, Clichy, Rosicky, Nasri, Song, Wilshere, Arshavin, Van Persie. Substitutes: Chamakh for Arshavin, Bendtner for Van Persie. Not used: Almunia, Squillaci, Eboue, Denilson.
Birmingham: Foster, Carr, Johnson, Ridgewell, Jiranek, Bowyer, Larsson, Gardner, Ferguson, Fahey, Zigic. Subsitutes: Beausejour for Gardner, Martins for Fahey, Jerome for Zigic. Not used: Taylor, Murphy, Parnaby, Phillips.
Referee: Mike Dean
Attendance: 88,851

Although they were underdogs, Birmingham were determined to prove they weren't going to be beaten on effort, determination or resilience. They harried and dogged the Gunners at every turn in the early stages, led by manager Alex McLeish. Arsenal with Cesc Fabregas and Theo Walcott missing through injury, were somewhat subdued and never hit their stride at Wembley. It was almost as if the occasion had got to them more than the travellers from the West Midlands.

From the start, Birmingham could have been a goal and a man ahead, after Lee Bowyer ran clear into the Gunners' box only to be felled by 'keeper Szczesny. It could and should have been a penalty, and if the letter of the law had been applied by referee Mike Dean, also a red card for the 'keeper. As it was, the North Londoners were reprieved by a flag from the linesman saving Dean from having to make such an early contentious decision. But if the Blues were frustrated at the incorrect call, they refused to show it, even after Arshavin could have added to their grievances with a snap shot that Foster did well to save on the turn. Foster was to have a fine game in goal, showing the potential he had shown only in glimpses at Old Trafford.

Yet it was to be the big Serbian Nicola Zigic, once linked with Arsenal, who put the Blues ahead on 28 minutes. Zigic, chosen for his obvious aerial threat to the Gunners at set pieces, evaded the attention of a clutch of red-and-white defenders, and Szczesny in the 6-yard area. The Serb used his height effectively to head into the net after Johnson's caused problems following a corner.

Zigic would have been annoyed at not doubling the lead shortly after, but his touch and technique let him down at the crucial moment, succeeding in helping Szczesny to block after useful play by Craig Gardner.

Yet for all Birmingham's resilience and attacking intent combined with hitherto defensive discipline, Arsenal showed the quality they had in abundance by levelling in the 39th minute. Hitchin-born Jack Wilshere thudded a shot against the Blues' upright from just outside the area after the St Andrews-based outfit neglected to clear. From the ensuing melee, Arshavin crossed for Van Persie, who had both feet in the air in anticipation of an airborne volley, which he struck expertly, athletically directing the ball past Foster's dive.

With the score at 1-1 it was game on, with the odds weighted in the Gunners favour due to the superior class and technique they possessed. The notion was confirmed further by Foster, who stopped a viciously swerving shot from Nasri as Dean blew the whistle on an entertaining first half. Many Arsenal fans in the crowd looked forward to the second-half with renewed vigour and expectation at a trophy after six long years. How wrong they would be.

With the second half nearly over and extra time looming later, substitute Obafemi Martins seized on a disastrous defensive mix-up on 88 minutes, leaving Birmingham City to acquire the first major honour since 1963.

Martins, on loan from the Russian Rubin Kazan, capitalised on a ruinous breakdown in communication between 'keeper Szczesny and defender Laurent Koscielny to net the late winner for the Blues, sending Arsenal fans at Wembley and around the globe into despair.

Martins, on for Keith Fahey, was left with the easiest of openings once Koscielny tried to clear as Szczesny moved to gather Nikola Zigic's soft header. It was a defensive calamity that reminded Gunners fans of a certain vintage of Gus Caesar's dreadful aborted effort to clear in the 1988 Rumbelows Cup final, which allowed Mark Stein to nip in and score the late winner in a 3-2 victory. Twenty-three years on, to many Arsenal fans it felt as if a cruel history had been repeated.

A visibly stunned Wenger commented after the game,

Making mistakes is not positive of course. I am bitterly disappointed, like the whole team. We had some problems to start the game, the number of games we played caught up a little bit on us. It took us a while to get into the rhythm and pace of the game. In the second half we were on top, unfortunately we couldn't score the second goal and, in the end, we made a mistake that left us no time at all to respond. We were preparing to play extra time.

Congratulations to Birmingham, they took advantage of the mistake [and] they took the trophy which hurts us tremendously. We have to be proud of our attitude, continue with our belief, pick ourselves up and face the other challenges we have. The team is very disappointed and we will face a lot of questions after that mistake tonight but we have to be strong enough to stand up. It is a good opportunity to show that we have the mental strength to respond to the situation like that.

It was a lack of communication, determination a little bit as well. Like always, when the ball is in no-man's land, someone has to take responsibility and go for it. What was amazing [was that] no one was going for the ball from Birmingham.

Both of them [Koscielny and Szczesny] are destroyed. I don't think it's a good moment for me to add anything. We have to lift them up again and help them, that is what a team is about. That is part of the game, we had enough chances to kill the game off before. They could only be dangerous, in the end, on free-kicks. Maybe we were a bit nervous on it as well. We don't deny it is a massive disappointment for the team.

We came here today to win the game, we didn't want to lose the game. In the last 18 games we lost one at Ipswich in the first leg of the Carling Cup [Semi-Final] and we lost today in the last minute on a very special goal. What the team is overall achieving is absolutely tremendous – that's why we go for every single game to win it. We are on such a long run that it is difficult to take because we are used to winning.

43

Manchester United (A)

28 August 2011

This was the game that arguably ended Arsène Wenger's hitherto unshakeable belief in youth. It was terribly sad the experiment borne out of necessity through the lean financial years that followed the club's move from Highbury to the Emirates – and one that somehow turned into a dogmatic mantra – was to meet with a humiliating end for such a noble, laudable and ground-breaking project.

Arsenal were unable to win either of their first two League games of the season. A 0-0 draw at St James's Park, with the actions of Joey Barton again being instrumental in provoking an Arsenal player into being sent off. This season it was the unfortunate Gervinho on his debut as the man in red and white player to take an early bath. A poor 2-0 defeat at home to a Kenny Dalglish-led Liverpool was mitigated by the club easing past the Italians of Udinese 3-1 on aggregate in the all-important Champions League third qualifying stage – crucially securing group stage football again for Wenger and the North Londoners for the fifteenth consecutive season. It was this praiseworthy achievement that gave Wenger a false sense of confidence in the days running up the fateful clash at Old Trafford.

As he said,

You could feel the tension in our side before the Udinese game. After the first game against Udinese, the squad was a bit insecure because we only won 1-0 and because of the quality of Udinese. That game was in our mind when we played against Liverpool. But that is out of the way now and I am confident you will see a much more convincing team against Manchester United. I am confident that we will be solid on Sunday and will have a good performance. It is vital for us to have a very good game on Sunday.

What will be important is the performance we put in on Sunday – to convince ourselves that we can play a part at the top level. But, of course, we don't want the gap to become too big. In our first part of the season, we play all the big teams away from home first. It is even more important to get results and not let Manchester United, for example, get away too early. I feel, since the start of the season, that we have a strong spirit and are highly determined. The response we gave in the second half against Udinese gives us a lot of strength and credit. It convinces me that this team has the ability to respond. And of course there is another opportunity to do that against Manchester United on Sunday. They are definitely still the team to beat. For us to beat them would be a great boost and would put us in a great position.

Unfortunately, they were words that would haunt Wenger.

Manchester United: De Gea, Evra, Jones, Evans, Smalling, Anderson, Nani, Young, Cleverley, Rooney, Welbeck. Substitutes: Park Ji-sung for Nani, Hernandez for Welbeck, Giggs for Anderson. Not used: Lindegaard, Ferdinand, Fabio Da Silva, Berbatov.
Arsenal: Szczesny, Koscielny, Djourou, Jenkinson, Traore, Rosicky, Walcott, Ramsey, Arshavin, Coquelin, Van Persie. Substitutes: Oxlade-Chamberlain for Coquelin, Lansbury for Walcott, Chamakh for Van Persie. Not used: Fabianski, Miquel, Ozyakup, Sunu.
Referee: Howard Webb
Attendance: 75,448

The Times led with the headline, 'Rooney leads slaughter of the innocents'. Match reporter Oliver Kay stated it was a 'demolition so emphatic and brutal ... a Sunday League scoreline and a Sunday League performance from Arsenal ... in a demoralised and depleted state.' The BBC's chief football writer Phil McNulty wrote, 'For Wenger it was a performance, or lack of one, that proved the folly of his summer of transfer inaction.'

Quite simply, Arsenal were annihilated at Old Trafford, suffering their heaviest defeat since the 8-0 loss away to Loughborough Town in 1896. It spoke volumes when Sir Alex Ferguson, Wenger's chief rival and protagonist in the first ten years of his reign, took pity on the Frenchman saying, 'We could have scored more goals, but you don't want to score more goals against a weakened team like that.' Such mercy was a sad indictment of how far Arsenal had fallen since winning the league in 2004 – and Wenger knew it.

Arsenal, who were three goals down to Welbeck, Young and Rooney before Walcott scored on the stroke of half-time to give false hope proceeded to fall apart in the second half. Nani and Park added strikes to go with a second for Young and two more for Rooney, including a penalty as United ran riot in the final third of the game, which would also see Jenkinson sent off for two fouls. Van Persie netted a late second for Arsenal, tempered by his first-half penalty miss, but in truth the only people associated with Arsenal who came away with any credit on this dark, dark day for the club were the visiting supporters, who showed true loyalty to the badge by loudly singing their support for the club and their side, even as the team fell apart. A fact sadly ignored by many who reported on the game.

A shell-shocked Wenger said afterwards,

You don't think like that after a game like this. It is terribly painful but you do not compare your pain. You have pain and that is it. I feel it was under very special circumstances. We have played three games in the Premier League and two Champions League games. It is not a time to make a balance of the whole season. Of course it hurts, it's humiliating, but you could see that we had not recovered physically in the second half from Wednesday night. We were short in some areas, for sure. They have class and they punished us. It was 3-1 at half-time and I think that was harsh against us. We missed a penalty, we had a chance to get back to 3-2. We tried desperately to get back but we opened ourselves up and were punished. Their finishing was great today.

I am very open if we can find the right players. We have the money to sign players. If we find players who can strengthen our team then we will do it. But I am not the only one to work on the case, we have 20 people who are working on that. If we do not do it, it is because we don't find them. We have plenty of players out today, too many players missing. We do not have the squad to compete when we have this many players out. At the moment, we have not found the solutions to our problems outside. When you look at today, you cannot predict how many players we have out. We did not expect to have Wilshere out, Diaby out, Gervinho out, Vermaelen out and Gibbs out. It is difficult to find excuses after a game like that. Wages-wise, of course we are behind the other teams.

When pressed on whether experience was needed he replied,

Yes but it is difficult when you lose 8-2. It is better when you don't talk as much but it hurts and it looks like you are looking for excuses. We have to sort out our problems that we have in the squad.

I am in a public job and I have to accept that. I try to make the right decisions for the Club and I will continue to do that. The players we have sold are players I brought to the Club. If you look at the 15 years I have been at the Club, I have brought in some good players. We have played three games in the Premier League, give me more time before saying that I have got it completely wrong. There were patches in the game where we had quality. I feel we collapsed physically more than anything else today.

In all, there were six players who were twenty-two years old or younger in the Arsenal team. However, the average age of Manchester United side was, in fact, younger – even if they did possess far more experience, experience that was desperately needed at a listing Arsenal.

The signing of five players only days later heralded the end of such an enterprising ambition in terms of Wenger's commitment to fielding youthful teams. A commitment that he had so stubbornly fought for in his unyielding manner for so long. He deserved better than the 8-2. But in reality, such a horrific result was perhaps needed to end his insistence on relying solely on youthful exuberance.

Never again would he field such a young side. But never again would he experience such a humiliating scoreline.

44

Leeds United (H)

9 January 2012

After Arsenal unexpectedly lost to Fulham 2-1 at Craven Cottage to a late Bobby Zamora goal in their first match of 2012, Wenger confirmed he would play a strong side against Leeds United in the FA Cup third round at the Emirates a week later. Yet when asked whether he had any singings up his sleeve, he responded by saying, 'At the moment nothing, we don't have a concrete case but we don't rule it out.'

The truth was Wenger and Ivan Gazidis were working closely behind the scenes with the New York Red Bulls and Major League Soccer to sensationally re-sign Arsenal legend and icon Thierry Henry for two months, to cover losing Gervinho and Marouane Chamakh, who were departing for Africa Cup of Nations duty.

Wenger speaking on the day the deal was done said,

I am very happy. It was my desire and Thierry's desire. We will have Thierry for January and in February. Then he will go back to the United States. I am sure during these two months he will be a massive asset to the team in the dressing room and on the pitch. He can be relaxed, not under too much pressure and be a tremendous help to the team.

Henry was originally signed for Arsenal from Juventus in August 1999 as a winger, before the alchemist Wenger transformed Henry into one of the world's greatest strikers. Henry was a vital member of the 2003/04 'Invincibles', who famously were unbeaten for a whole thirty-eight-match season. In his eight years in North London playing for 'the club of his life' (1999–2007), he picked up two Premier League Championships, two FA Cups, the Premier League Golden Boot on four occasions and the PFA Player of the Year twice. On 7 May 2006, he scored the last-ever goal at Highbury.

In all, Henry made 370 appearances for the Gunners, scoring 226 goals, making him the club's all-time leading scorer. The club marked their 125th anniversary by unveiling a statue cast in bronze of Henry showing his never-to-be-forgotten celebration after scoring against Spurs at Highbury in November 2002.

Of his return that had supporters reminiscing over his glorious Arsenal career, Henry said,

It is unreal to be honest. But when it comes to Arsenal my heart will always do the talking. Once I knew the plan behind it I was OK with it. I am not coming here to be a hero or prove anything. I am just coming here to help. People have to understand that. Marouane and Gervinho are going to the Africa Cup of Nations, so I was asked to fill in the gap. It is a loan deal and I'll be on the bench most of the time. If I can make the bench that is! The

Boss has a team here already who are doing something good. I am just going to be part of the squad.

Henry added, 'It is hard for me when it comes to Arsenal. I am not coming here for the whole season ... I hope it is a win-win situation where I can help Arsenal and come back fit for the MLS season.'

For Arsenal fans, the night Henry returned to Arsenal was more than a win-win situation – it was watching the return of a living legend, and how they celebrated the fact.

Arsenal: Szczesny, Coquelin, Koscielny, Squillaci, Miquel, Song, Ramsey, Arteta, Oxlade-Chamberlain, Arshavin, Chamakh. Substitutes: Yennaris on for Coquelin, Walcott for Arshavin, Henry for Chamakh. Not used: Martinez, Benayoun, Miyaichi, Park.
Leeds United: Lonergan, Lees, Thompson, O'Dea, White, Clayton, Vayrynen, Pugh, Townsend, Becchio, Nunez. Substitutes: Brown for Vayrynen, McCormack for Becchio, Forsell for Nunez. Not used: Taylor, Bruce, Sam, Parker.
Attendance: 59,615

The game was deadlocked 0-0 when Thierry Henry came on in the 68th minute to a reception fit for a king. In truth it was for a king – the King of Highbury. Yet Henry, managed to add some more history to the legend that the majority of Arsenal fans had thought ended in 2007, and this time it would be at the Emirates. Within ten minutes of reappearing in Arsenal colours in his second coming, Thierry had sent the crowd into paroxysms of joy, unmatched, as many regulars said, by anything else that season.

Henry, showing all his nous and streetwise ability to pull away from his marker, as if it was 2004 all over again, controlled Alex Song's pass, before ghosting into the box, opening up his chest and the angle of his body before slotting the ball past a stunned Lonegran. The celebrations were as powerful as they were intense as every Gooner in the ground – and on the planet – jumped for joy at such a resonant and evocative act. Henry himself, overcome with emotion, beat his chest in utter happiness before running to embrace Wenger. And as the North Londoners triumphed 1-0 at the final whistle, King Henry raised his hands to the heavens and shed a tear – just as he did when his statue was unveiled outside the ground a month previously.

The result saw the Gunners play Aston Villa in the fourth round of the FA Cup. But the significance – in terms of a true returning hero Wenger re-signed providing another moment of joy after five years of being away – was, for many watching fans, the highlight of the season.

Wenger said afterwards with a wide grin, 'It was the perfect script from a perfectly special player. It showed that some things never die like class, motivation and desire to win. Thierry has shown that tonight.'

Henry, his eyes welling up with emotion at what had just occurred, said modestly,

I am not 25 anymore, I am not going to take the ball from the middle of the park and dribble past five or six players. I remember Dennis Bergkamp used to be the main front guy. Suddenly he was playing behind the striker and if you have the awareness to see things before other players, you can get away with not having your legs.

When the boss spoke to me about coming back, I wanted to make sure I didn't disturb the team that was in place. That was important to me, I am a fan don't forget that. I know people want silverware, but you have to think about the long term and what they have been doing for a very long time is amazing. I'm not coming back here to be a hero or prove anything, I'm coming here to help.

It's kind of unreal to be honest, it's all happened so fast. I came to the decision that I was going to come back here to help, it was going to be a loan deal. It was kind of a weird one and it did happen pretty fast but when it comes down to Arsenal it's pretty hard for me to say no. If you ask anybody if they want to help the team they love and support, it was difficult for me to say no knowing the part I was going to play.

Wenger said,

You cannot take away from people what they have done, and what he has delivered will stay forever. It can just make the statue a bit bigger! Let's hope he will do that.

I just told him where he plays, because he can play on the flanks or through the middle. I told him to play through the middle. He did not know who was coming off. For the rest, you don't need to tell him too much. He has seen it all and done it all. You could see when he came on he had a presence on the pitch and if we could find him, he would be dangerous. He was sharp physically. He did well. Straight away through his runs he made them drop a little bit deeper. Once he was caught offside, once the centre back intercepted the ball, but he has a kind of presence. His movement gives defenders a problem. After 10 minutes on the pitch he knows where to go – he was already a legend here and now has added a bit more to the story.

Wenger added he wasn't surprised by Henry's magical feat,

No, because already in training I have seen that he was sharp and ready to play. I would not put him on the pitch with what he has done here if he was not ready because that would be unfair. He is a special player. What is good for the young players at the club is that a guy who has done it all comes and prepares 100 per cent, warms-up, is focused and motivated, and comes on with an immense desire to do well.

Still you feel he has some pressure. Thierry is a proud guy, he does not want to disappoint people. He knows he will be compared to what he has done before. That is what champions are about. They always say 'I have no pressure', but they want to be seen as people who do well. It is a kind of a comeback and you know you want that to be a success as a player.

You can accuse me of many things, but not that I kicked Thierry Henry out, because he wanted to go. I explained that many times. I was always happy to get him back.

Wenger's final comment summed up the night – an evening for the ages with an unashamedly romantic, sentimental, life-affirming ending that would be savoured by every Arsenal fan – by saying,

Yes, it was a little bit of a dream, because it was a story about football you would tell some young children. Unfortunately it is not often like that in our game, but sometimes it happens.

When he got in that position I thought 'oh, that's your angle' but it was a bit too close. That's where he surprised me. He still didn't force the shot, he still made it look easy, where I would have expected him to take a very strong inside shot. He made it just look easy. At the start I thought he was too much on the left but he had that special finishing that he has shown tonight.

That was the Thierry Henry finishing.

On a night bursting with emotion, another Thierry Henry finish gave everyone something to remember for a very long time.

45

Tottenham Hotspur (H)
26 February 2012

Following Arsenal's defeats to Sunderland in the FA Cup and a humbling 4-0 in the San Siro to AC Milan in the Champions League first knockout stage, and with the club being a worrying ten points off Spurs in fourth place, Arsène Wenger said,

> Every game is massive now until the end of the season, but it is exciting. What is terrible is to play a game of no importance. What is important is we enjoy it and come out with a good performance. I don't know if this is my most important derby. For us it is important because we have an opportunity to come back closer to Spurs and strengthen our position in fourth place, which is a very important target.
>
> You judge who are top at the end of the season, not in February. The only thing you can say is that in the last 15 years Spurs have finished behind Arsenal. We want to respect everybody. We will respect Tottenham on Sunday and we want our players and supporters to be respected as well.

After the memorable 90 minutes that occurred, with the Gunners playing scintillating football, Tottenham's players, and fans – many of whom turned up in London Transport style T-shirts that read 'Mind The Gap' – suddenly found a new respect of their red-and-white rivals in a game never-to-be-forgotten by Gooners everywhere.

At 2-0 down the Gunners and Wenger were staring into an abyss. A thirteen-point abyss. Yet what followed was a comeback of hugely satisfying proportions that immediately entered the annals of North London derby history, and had the majority of Spurs fans leaving long before the final whistle.

Arsenal: Szczesny, Sagna, Koscielny, Vermaelen, Gibbs, Song, Arteta, Rosicky, Walcott, Benayoun, van Persie. Substitutes: Jenkinson for Gibbs, Oxlade-Chamberlain for Walcott, Gervinho for Benayoun. Not used: Fabianski, Miquel, Park, Chamakh.
Tottenham Hotspur: Friedel, Walker, King, Kaboul, Assou-Ekotto, Kranjcar, Parker, Modric, Bale, Saha, Adebayor. Substitutes: Van der Vaart for Saha, Sandro for Kranjcar, Dawson for King. Not used: Cudicini, Rose, Lennon, Defoe.
Referee: Mike Dean
Attendance: 60,106

Louis Saha opened the scoring with a goal that entered the net via a wicked deflection off Vermaelen before looping over a stranded Szczesny on four minutes. With 34 minutes gone, the hated ex-Arsenal forward Adebayor made it 2-0 with a contentious penalty that should not have been awarded after the future Real Madrid winger Gareth Bale went down far too easily after Arsenal's Polish 'keeper came out to smother the ball.

Within seven minutes of going 2-0 down, Arsenal showed not only their large reserves of talent but more importantly in a North London derby, large reserves of grit, character and a refusal to give in.

Thankfully, Arteta on 40 minutes crossed for an attacking Bacary Sagna to steer the ball into the net with an unlikely header. Three minutes later, van Persie made it 2-2 with a curling top corner effort. The momentum had suddenly been regained by Arsenal and Tomas Rosicky, who was having his best game of the season, put the Pride of North London 3-2 up.

The lead was never to be clawed back by the shell-shocked visitors. The Czech, who led by example with his unceasing desire to win this North London derby for his club, then fed Walcott a through ball that the winger cum forward slotted home at the near post to send the Emirates wild. The scoring was not over yet, as Walcott led a by now punch-drunk Lilywhites defence a merry dance before netting number five.

To crown a miserable day for the visitors from N17, Scott Parker was then sent off in the 87th minute, serenaded by a sea of red cards that were the home fans' season tickets. For Arsène Wenger, it capped a remarkable comeback in a remarkable game that Gunners fans would always remember.

As David Hynter said in his *Guardian* report the next morning,

This was a North London derby in keeping with the season's scarcely credible story-lines... as the visitors, departed with a dent to their pride and their aspirations to finish as London's top club ... [and] a triumph to make the Arsenal support forget their misgivings.

Wenger reflected on the turnaround in his post-match press conference saying,

Arsenal are alive more than anybody thought before the game. Today we gave a performance that on the spirit side, the technical side, the drive of the whole team, on the style of the game we want to play everything was perfect despite a very bad start. I felt in the first five minutes Tottenham started well, after that it was all us for 85 minutes.

We were always on top of the game. We were 2-0 down but refused to lose the game and kept going no matter what happened. Once we were back to 2-2 you could see that if we maintained the pace, we would win the game. We had a good balance between offence and defence, between creativity and going into the space behind the defenders and good maturity.

We had a great spirit. I must say the way we want to play football depends on the pitch and this was the first time in three games that we played on a football pitch that is really a football pitch. That helps as well.

I felt that Theo Walcott had the qualities that, considering the rest of the team, are highly needed. He is a player who can be straight and go behind the defenders – nobody else is like that. He is a very direct player, he can sometimes miss a first touch but considering the balance of the team I thought it was important to keep him in the side.

For the first goal we were caught on the counter attack and the second was not a penalty. We played against a team with Saha, Adebayor, Gareth Bale, Modric – you cannot dream they do not get any chance at all in the 90 minutes.

They felt flooded in the middle of the park and couldn't get to the ball. They tried to stop us from dominating the midfield but it didn't stop us. I felt we were technically faster and superior in our passing.

I was pleased with the drive, enthusiasm and the refusal to lose at any cost of my team today. That has been questioned about the team, so I am very proud. Yes I feel they answered their critics. You could see there was exceptional spirit there. They are always under a lot of criticism but when everyone is fit you can see that we are a good side.

As Arsenal and Wenger had pulled the points deficit back to a far more manageable seven points, suddenly those 'Mind The Gap' T-shirts sported by crowing Spurs fans didn't seem like such a good idea.

46

Reading (A)

30 October 2012

Arsène Wenger was delighted to see the 'special' Jack Wilshere return, after a seventeen-month lay-off, for the 1-0 win against QPR at the Emirates the previous Saturday.

People have to be a little bit patient to see the best of him again. Even if he's not 100 per cent today, he still shows in aspects of the game that he is a classy player. He was cheered a lot, but I don't think it was because people expected too much of him. It was just a happiness that he was back.

He is special. People who understand football understand that he is a good player. He has that typical thing where he can turn and take the ball forward, which is very difficult for a midfielder. He still lacks a little bit of ability to get away from people, but he will get that. Jack is a great player – however he will only be great if the team is great.

Wenger had also spoken at the club's AGM the week, before outlining his priorities in terms of silverware:

The Capital One Cup comes in a period where you have to make a decision sometimes, as it is a time when we also have the league and the Champions League. I gave a frank and honest opinion about where the priorities are. But you want to do well in all the competitions in which you play.

We will go to Reading with a good team who will have a good chance to win the game. Some players need a breather because they had two international games, the Champions League and Premier League games. They will have played five games in two weeks so some will be rested. But everything is open, for every game we can change the selection of the players.

Reading have done well over the years, and they have done especially well in their scouting. They are one of the examples of living within their resources. I always respect that. There is some quality work behind their success. And you have to congratulate Brian McDermott for promotion last year, I believe he made a miracle basically.

They are a tough team. They will be difficult to beat so it will be a big test for us.

After the game at the Madjeski, Wenger's last comments were to be the understatement of the season.

Arsenal: Martinez, Jenkinson, Djourou, Koscielny, Miquel, Coquelin, Frimpong, Gnabry, Walcott, Arshavin, Chamakh. Substitutes: Eisfeld for Frimpong, Giroud for Gnabry, Meade for Miquel. Not used: Shea, Squillaci, Bellerin, Yennaris.

Reading: Federici, Gunter, Shorey, Gorkss, Morrison, Tabb, Leigertwood, McCleary, Robson-Kanu, Hunt, Roberts. Substitutes: McAnuff for McLeary, Pogrebnyak for Hunt, Church for Roberts. Not used: Taylor, Harte, Pearce, Le Fondre.
Referee: Kevin Friend
Attendance: 23,980

The *Telegraph*'s Henry Winter wrote of the night's events in disbelief,

> This was one of the epic cup ties, an emotion-shredder of a match that saw the Mad Stad live up to its nickname as Arsenal amazingly recovered from 4-0 down to reach the quarter-finals of the Capital One Cup… it was the type of comeback that had Arsenal fans looking at each other in disbelief and delight. Many will be hoarse this morning, having sung in anger and joy. Arsenal fans left with priceless memories.

With 37 minutes gone, the Gunners were an improbable 4-0 down and out in Reading, Berkshire. Goals from Jason Roberts, Laurent Koscielny's own goal, Mikele Leigertwood and Noel Hunt sent Royals fans into wonderland they scarcely believed possible. If Walcott hadn't netted just before half-time, it is debatable Arsenal would have scored a goal on the night. As it was, Giroud hit a second midway through the second half to give the 5,000 travelling Gooners hope. But on 89 minutes, the score still remained 4-2 to Reading. Yet Koscielny made amends for his earlier own goal to hit the third with only a minute left before, incredibly, Walcott swept home a leveller to draw the North Londoners level at 4-4 with only seconds of injury time left.

The drama didn't end there either.

Marouane Chamakh and Pavel Pogrebnyak both hit the back of the net to make it 5-5, with penalties looming large, before Walcott made it a hat-trick in the 120th minute before Chamakh fired home his second and Arsenal's seventh away goal on the night, making the final scoreline a breathless if rabidly entertaining 7-5.

For many Arsenal fans, it was the most mind-boggling game of football they had ever watched. As Henry Winter said in the next morning's *Telegraph*, 'As the years pass, they will always recall events of last night. This is what following a team is all about, the ambushing of the emotions, the lows and the highs, the sublime replacing the ridiculous.'

Wenger, mindful of the calamity that was only narrowly avoided, was rather more circumspect after the game:

> We went from disaster to, I must say at least at some stage, pride – because we at least came back in the second half with a decent performance. We had just hope but it didn't look like we would go through. At least in the second half, we got our disastrous first half out of the system. Then, once it was 4-4, I think it looked like we would be the winner of the game. Reading had given a lot, and were mentally down, and in extra time the maximum they could have got was a penalty shoot-out. We looked quite comfortable in the second half. Reading had a fantastic first half. I know what it is to be pulled back when you're 4-0 up. It happened to me as well. They should take credit from that performance and not be too disappointed.
>
> At 4-1, I thought we had a chance. In the second half we played 4-2-4, basically 4-1-5. We created many chances and, from then on, I always had hope we could come back.

We had some free-kicks around the box but we couldn't score. With 15 minutes to go, I thought that's the moment to score the 4-3. We didn't. Seven minutes to go, we had a great chance. We didn't take it. It's strange to explain. At 4-0, you think you have won the game. At 4-1 you still think you have won the game. At 4-2, you suddenly realise that it's not over - and then the panic kicks in and no matter how good a player you are, that goes through the team.

At 4-0 I didn't feel great. I just thought 'what can I do about that?' I started to think about my half-time speech. It was not difficult to find an inspiration at half-time because there was enough there to talk about. Overall, I just felt sorry for our fans because at 2-0, they stayed behind the team. At 3-0, they stayed behind the team. At 4-0, they stayed behind the team. I would like to give them credit tonight. I'm happy we paid them back in the second half.

When asked if the match was one of his greatest ever victories he replied,

Maybe, yes. It is not one of our priorities but had we gone out the way we could have gone out in the first-half would not have been one of my proudest moments at the Club.

I'm very happy that we responded the way we did in the second.

So were the 5,000 travelling Arsenal fans who watched this incredible game.

47

Tottenham Hotspur (H)

17 November 2012

Arsène Wenger spoke ahead of the North London derby by talking about the importance Jack Wilshere placed on the game:

> Jack arrived here at the age of nine years old and that means this game is in his heart, in his brain, for the whole season every year – from the youth teams up, the rivalry exists. Every London derby is important. As well, we dropped some points recently and we want to come back in a more consistent way of results. The distance is not big between us and them. It's early in the season. First of all, we play at the Emirates. We know that it's important we are strong there. As well, for us, a successful season is down to consistency of results. At the moment that's what we are looking for.

When asked were his North London rivals getting closer every year, in the knowledge that the Gunners had finished above their bitter rivals for seventeen consecutive seasons, Wenger replied with a wry smile,

> I get that question every year. For some time, we were winning championships and they were not in the top four at all, so of course they've got closer in recent years. But fortunately we managed always to get above them. However, our main target is to finish above Tottenham. Our main target is to finish at least in the top four. To be in the top four it is important to beat Tottenham and it also has an emotional impact.
>
> What affects me is that our fans are not happy. It doesn't stop me from doing what I do on the football pitch, but if you ask me, my biggest desire is to see our fans happy – like the players as well. It's important in the end to have consistency, and certainly the results in the two derbies can have a big influence as well on the qualifying spots for the Champions League.

This derby certainly played a big part in determining one of the qualifying spots for the Champions League.

Arsenal: Szczesny, Sagna, Koscielny, Mertesacker, Vermaelen, Arteta, Wilshere, Cazorla, Walcott, Podolski, Giroud. Substitutes: Ramsey for Wilshere, Santos for Podolski, Oxlade-Chamberlain for Giroud. Not used: Mannone, Jenkinson, Coquelin, Arshavin.
Tottenham Hotpur: Lloris, Walker, Gallas, Vertonghen, Naughton, Huddlestone, Sandro, Lennon, Bale, Defoe, Adebayor. Substitutes: Dempsey for Naughton, Dawson for Walker, Carroll for Huddlestone. Not used: Friedel, Livermore, Townsend, Sigurdsson.

Referee: Howard Webb
Attendance: 60,111

Arsenal fans could have been forgiven for thinking that it was Groundhog Day in this particular North London derby, nine months on from the first 5-2 win of 2012. The Gunners again came from behind to register a second stunning 5-2 evisceration of their hated rivals, who once again showed their indiscipline to finish with ten men.

Jason Birt writing in the *Telegraph* after the match said,

> At this rate Emmanuel Adebayor will become a hate figure on both sides of North London. Having baited his former club in comments published on Saturday morning before scoring against them at lunchtime – inevitably celebrating in front of the Arsenal supporters – he was then quickly dismissed for a lunge at Santi Cazorla that turned this derby match on its head and spoiled what was shaping up to be an epic encounter.

Arsène Wenger added emphatically,

> It was not a rose, it was not a yellow – it was red. Tottenham again had a good start, we were a bit nervous and scored one goal when we made an adjustment mistake at the back, and a chance for a second goal. It looked like last season's game, but then there was the turning point with the sending off of Adebayor.

It was indeed as his 17th minute expulsion saw the game swing decisively in the Gunners' favour as Per Mertesacker, Lukas Podolski and Olivier Giroud turned the game on its head before the first 45 minutes had elapsed.

As Wenger said,

> It certainly changed the game because Adebayor had a good start, he was lively. But I didn't think at all when he was sent off that the game was won. We came back into the game and got what we wanted, which was to win the game. It is not always easy against 10 – we have won games with 10 men. I thought it could become even more difficult because they could have dropped back and waited for us, but we had the quality and movement to play through their lines and create chances. There were some outstanding individual offensive performances. In the second half you could see that the confidence was not completely still there, I hope that this result will help us.

Cazorla added a fourth for a rampant Arsenal before Bale pulled it back to 4-2 which was only a prelude to Walcott netting a fifth on 90 minutes. Wenger added proudly shortly after the final whistle: 'This team has something special - they want to do well and they have quality. We have to find stability in our expression and we need some more time to work on that, but there's something special in the team.

When questioned on the Spurs' managers debatable claims, the Lilywhites were the better team he responded with as much sardonic irony as he could muster: 'If our opponents are in control from the first to the last minutes and we win 5-2, then I don't mind too much.'

Arsenal fans throughout the globe didn't mind either, including Jack Wilshere.

48

Newcastle United (H)

29 December 2012

Arsène Wenger spoke of Theo Walcott impressing him as a central striker, and hinted he would be granted more opportunities in the role. The England international had been voluble in his yearning to play as a centre-forward through the middle. The twenty-three-year-old had made a positive impression in his previous two games at Reading and Wigan Athletic in that position, and Wenger suggested prior to the Newcastle home match he would be tempted to employ him as the focal point of Arsenal's forward line.

Wenger said,

I like the signs that I have seen. If you look at my statements, I always said that one day he would play through the middle and it grew in his brain. He is now 23. I decided to play Thierry Henry at 23 through the middle because you have to learn a lot before. The fact that you play in other positions as well helps your technique. On the wing you need a shorter technique against the line. Once you [then] play in the middle you can go on both sides.

From 19 to 23, Theo has learnt a lot. Now we will sometimes play him on the flanks and sometimes through the middle. I like what I have seen through the middle. He has played two games at centre forward and you have to be open-minded in our job and give people a chance – if they take it, it's good. If not, he will still be a fantastic winger so it puts some more assets in his game.

He will learn something in his position and I am confident he will do well in that position. It's a bit early to compare him to Thierry Henry. Yes Thierry Henry gives him advice. It's always important. Theo is a very intelligent boy. He understands very quickly when you tell him something and that's why I think he can do very well in this position.

Wenger's faith in Walcott as a centre-forward was proved to be correct in this crazy game, which summed up everything that was good (and bad) about Arsenal that season.

Arsenal: Szczesny, Sagna, Koscielny, Vermaelen, Gibbs, Arteta, Wilshere, Cazorla, Oxlade-Chamberlain, Walcott, Podolski. Substitutes: Coquelin for Cazorla, Giroud for Oxlade-Chamberlain, Ramsey for Podolski. Not used: Rosicky, Djourou, Mannone, Gervinho.
Newcastle United: Krul, Simpson, Perch, Coloccini, Santon, Tiote, Cisse, Birgirimana, Marveaux, Obertan, Ba. Substitutes: Ferguson for Simpson, Shola Ameobi for Birgirimana, Tavernier for Marveaux. Not used: Sammy Ameobi, Harper, Abeid, Street.
Referee: Chris Foy
Attendance: 60,087

This game encapsulated why the Premier League is the most watched league in the world. With constant attacking from both sides, to look away was to miss some action – entertainment resulting in ten goals from six different scorers. However, it also emphasised the defensive frailties preventing Arsenal from being viable challengers for the League title – once again.

With the visitors matching the Gunners blow for blow, until they succumbed to tiredness from the incessant attacking from North Londoners and Theo Walcott in particular, the scene was set for an upset of sorts at the Emirates – until the Berkshire-born winger (or was it now centre-forward?) produced a sublime performance ranking among the best by an individual in the Wenger reign. Walcott, who scored a hat-trick as well as producing two assists, said afterwards, 'I was very happy with my performance which showed what I am capable of at centre forward.'

Yet it could have been so different if Newcastle hasn't run out of steam shortly after Demba Ba had brought the North Easterners level at 3-3 in the 69th minute, as Arsenal smashed four goals in the remaining 21 minutes.

Even Arsène Wenger thought the result flattered his side confessing, 'The result was not an accurate indication of the match. We suffered for big parts in the game, especially in the first half. We were a bit nervous and had problems winning the ball back from them.'

The match started in brisk fashion as Ba, who had previously been linked with a transfer to Wenger's team opened the scoring in the 16th minute. Walcott then hinted at what was to come when he was provided with his first chance of the game four minutes later, responding to a Podolski through ball. By beating a poorly timed Magpies offside trap, he struck a low shot beyond Geordie 'keeper Tim Krul from 15 yards to make it 1-1. Ba then netted to make it 2-1 to the visitors two minutes before the break, as his free-kick from 20 yards took a significant deflection off the unfortunate Jack Wilshere past Szczesny.

Arsenal commenced the second-half with far more verve and were rewarded five minutes later by Alex Oxlade-Chamberlain, who fired decisively home from an accurate cross from Spaniard Santi Carzorla. Yet Newcastle equalised again with a goal that explained why Arsenal's defensive lapses would cost them dear over the course of the season. Gabriel Obertan swanned his way into the Gunners' box, pushing the ball across the face of goal. Sylvan Marveaux found himself very much alone at a deserted back post, and much to his surprise fired in from 2 yards as Wenger's defenders stood and glared at one another.

Or as Paul Doyle phrased it in the next morning's *Observer*, 'perplexed Arsenal defenders looked accusingly at each other [but] the confusion soon switched to the other end.' When Wilshere robbed Cheik Tiote in the middle, and went on to swap passes with Podolski before driving on and aiming a tantalising cross at the back post, the Argentine Coloccini only managed to nod it onto the woodwork as Podolski rushed on to head it into the net to make it 3-2.

The game was warming up nicely for Arsenal fans and Theo Walcott, if not Wenger's silent wish for a solid defensive display as, yet again, the Gunners defenders served up comical defending. As left-back Gibbs lost concentration, the effective Marveaux centred for Ba to volley efficiently past a despairing Szczesny to bring the scores level at 3-3. But that was without factoring in the magical twenty minutes Walcott had at the end. The speedster received a pass from another forward who had an excellent game, namely Podolski, and slotted the ball calmly home to make it 4-3. Olivier Giroud then arrived on the pitch, rendering Walcott's time in the middle over as he reverted to his more familiar right-wing berth. Walcott showed he could be just as effective out wide by crossing for the Frenchman to emphatically head past Krul. It was 6-3 shortly afterwards, after yet another mazy run by Theo resulted in Giroud netting again.

However, the best was saved until stoppage time, as Walcott embarked on a mesmerising run down the flank. He then cut inside and jinked past tired, weary and embarrassed Newcastle defenders patently wishing for the final whistle, avoiding a foul that would have resulted in a penalty, before keeping his composure and firing unequivocally past the hapless Krul to make the scoreline an improbable 7-3.

As Wenger noted afterwards,

We couldn't see any sign of giving up, even at 3-3. It's not easy, mentally. You cannot win every game 7-3. Your team has to be capable to sometimes win 1-0.

I don't know why we have had so many high-scoring games. People have been very impatient with us. We have rebuilt a team. We started well. We stuttered a little bit after and now we have come back. We had to rebuild a team and we have done it. [It] demands some time and some understanding. We still have some work to do.

As for Walcott's contribution, Wenger added impishly,

I like the fact Theo can play through the middle because it gives us more opportunities to do that and more possibilities to change from game to game. I will do it again. I have worked with Theo for seven years and the fact that he had an exceptional game today will not influence me more or less.

49

Aston Villa (H)
17 August 2013

At the start of his eighteenth season in charge of Arsenal, Arsène Wenger was well versed in dealing with questions of why he appeared to be reluctant to purchase new players.

Responding defiantly he said,

> Why should I resist? I just defend the idea you spend the money you have and not the money you don't have. For years I did that. Today we have more so we can spend more. It's as simple as that.
>
> Of course I am excited by that prospect but what I want to convince you of is that we are ready to spend the money if we feel that the players makes us a better team tomorrow morning. It's about the team, the quality of the play, the spirit and togetherness and the quality of the players. Therefore we have to focus on all the rest as well.

Yet he added,

> I don't disagree that we are a bit light at the moment – but it's not a question of spending the money, it's a question of finding the right players. We are not scared to spend money. But we want the right players. I understand every frustration, you have so many frustrated people, but what is important is the quality of what you do on the pitch, so let's not create a crisis from nothing.
>
> We look more for quality than for numbers. The first request is to have the quality to play for Arsenal FC, after the number comes in. Yes, we would like two or three players if possible but we will not compromise on the quality of the players.

Unfortunately, at the end of the his first 90 minutes of the new term, to say the fans were looking forward to the rest of the season would have been to underestimate the depth of feeling that had been aroused by this defining defeat. A defeat that signalled a change in transfer policy – hopefully placating a number of disgruntled fans.

Arsenal: Szczesny, Sagna, Mertesacker, Koscielny, Gibbs, Ramsey, Rosicky, Walcott, Wilshere, Oxlade-Chamberlain, Giroud. Substitutes: Jenkinson for Gibbs, Cazorla for Oxlade-Chamberlain, Podolski for Sagna. Not used: Frimpong, Gnabry, Podolski, Sanogo.
Aston Villa: Guzan, Lowton, Vlaar, Baker, Luna, El Ahmadi, Westwood, Delph, Agbonlahor, Weimann, Benteke. Substitutes: Clark for Baker, Bacuna for Weimann. Not used: Steer, Okore, Tonev, Helenius, Bowery.

Referee: Anthony Taylor
Attendance: 60,003

The ever-excellent Amy Lawrence wrote in her *Observer* match report,

> If you are not prepared to pay the price, there is a price to be paid. Arsenal's miserly summer, which finds them in transfer profit, ended in an opening-day loss. Aston Villa were organised, determined, took advantage of a couple of controversial calls by the referee, Anthony Taylor, and inflicted upon Arsenal a defeat that was both damaging and damning.
>
> Arsenal were a picture of deflation. The soundtrack as the crowd exited of wanting some money to be spent spoke volumes about how expectations are being undermined by a strategically inept transfer window.

It was hard to think of a more disappointing start to an Arsenal season in the Premier League era, if you discounted a shock 0-3 defeat by a Mick Quinn hat-trick for Coventry City, which was coincidentally the last opening-day home defeat. It was certainly the most discouraging one under Wenger's tenure.

The frustration the fans, the team and Wenger felt was compounded by their bright start. Arsenal took the lead as early as the sixth minute, when Tomas Rosicky fed Alex Oxlade-Chamberlain down the left flank, who crossed for an unmarked Olivier Giroud, who fired past Villa 'keeper Brad Guzan to put the Gunners 1-0 up. For those of a red and white persuasion, it was to be the day's high point.

Gabby Agbonlahor, who was lively all afternoon, slipped the ball between Koscielny's legs to nudge it past Szczesny, who subsequently pulled him down. The referee, Anthony Taylor, then played an advantage but, after Weimann fired his shot into the side netting, awarded a penalty.

Arsenal's Polish 'keeper managed to save from Benteke – but the powerful centre-forward showed anticipation by reaching the bouncing rebound to head home convincingly.

There was more anguish for Wenger and the fans in the second half. On 62 minutes, Cazorla lost the ball to Agbonlahor, who went to accelerate past Koscielny in the box. The French international slid in, appearing to get a substantial part of his foot on the ball, yet the official Taylor awarded a second penalty to Villa. Benteke made no mistake from the spot second time around and sent Szczesny the wrong way to make it 2-1.

The mutterings increased as Koscielny capped a game to forget by picking up a second yellow card when he fouled Weimann moments later.

On 86 minutes, Luna ran through to score Villa's third on the day as the ball evaded Szczesny before rebounding off the post and into the goal.

The game ended in acrimony with boos raining down from the stands from some fans, and others demanding money be spent on transfers. More fans stood in stunned silence, disturbed by what could be described as the first signs of civil war between supporters.

Amy Lawrence ended her match report with a nod to the lack of transfer activity emanating from the club: 'A banner hanging from the upper tier read: "You can't buy class." The last word seemed somewhat redundant.'

However, immediately after the game Wenger said, looking as dejected as he had ever done during his time at Arsenal,

It's a big disappointment to lose a game like that.

We started the game well and then suddenly everything went against us and in the end we lost 3-1 so it is a big blow and even when we had 10 men we had chances to come back to 2-2.

When asked again by a reporter why money had not yet been spent on adding to the squad he replied feistily,

I can return your question. Could we have won the game with the players that were on the pitch today? That's for me the real question. And I say yes. After that, if we do not spend the money, it's because we do not find the players. I'm not the only one to work on that. We are a team who work on that.

We are ready to buy the players if we find that the players are good enough for us. That's all we can tell you.

Wenger also had a heartfelt message for the fans, who pleaded for him to spend some money on additions:

Yes, I can understand the fans' frustrations. We want our fans to be happy. When you don't achieve that, you feel absolutely sorry and really disappointed when the fans are not happy.

My job is to make the fans happy. We haven't lost the game because of that. That's what I just want to convince you of. That we are on the market, everybody knows that we are ready to buy players. Everybody knows.

In 16 years, I've shown my loyalty to this Club. My worry is to do well. That's the only worry. As long as I'm here, I want to do well. I'm absolutely hugely disappointed. It's a massive blow and that's why the solution is not to sit here and say, 'Yes we'll buy and keep you happy.'

I'm not here to say who is right and who is wrong. I'm here to make people happy who love this Club. When we don't do it, I feel sorry. I have to look at the solution at the start of the game. We couldn't go out at five to three and buy six players. When the game starts, you have to win the game. Could we win the game with the players we have? I say yes.

After, we are out to buy players. People always say 'buy players, buy players, buy players'. When you tell them 'tell me who?' it becomes much more problematic.

Whatever fans' views on the worrying saga it was clear to all – including Wenger and the board – signings had to be made.

On transfer deadline day, £42 million was spent on Real Madrid's playmaker Mesut Ozil. It was a capture that lifted the whole club and supporters in a deal that smashed the previous transfer record into smithereens, and signalled that Wenger and Arsenal were back as one of the big boys in the transfer market.

It was a signing that was intended to help bring some silverware back to the club by the season's finale to end nine long years of hurt – prompted by one of the most dispiriting matches in recent Arsenal history on and off the pitch.

50

Hull City (N)

17 May 2014

With fourth place safely secured, along with the prospect of Champions League football for the seventeenth year in succession, a trip to Wembley in glorious May sunshine beckoned. With such an appealing prospect to be savoured by the Arsenal fans off to Wembley, in the scandalously low allocation of 21,000, it was hard to recall the rancour generated by the League opener against Aston Villa nine months previously.

The Cup run started against Spurs in a third round North London derby, in which the wily Wenger made new Lilywhites manager Tim Sherwood look distinctly second best. Goals from Santi Cazorla and the evergreen Tomas Rosicky proved North London was red as they completed the second of three wins out of three against their hapless rivals, whose stillborn season never truly recovered after selling Gareth Bale to Real Madrid. The match was also memorable for dashing winger Theo Walcott, signalling the score to the travelling Tottenham fans while being carried past them on a stretcher – who then took umbrage by cowardly pelting him and his stretcher bearers with a hail of small change. Unfortunately, for the in-form winger, it was to be his last contribution of the season as a scan the next day discovered he had injured his cruciate ligament, ruling him out for the rest of the year, including a trip to Brazil.

Troubled Coventry City were the visitors on a Friday night fourth-round game. Arsenal fans, to their credit, showed solidarity with the Sky Blues' ownership problems and ground problems by clapping them at various significant points during the game. It was a gesture much appreciated by the long-suffering away support. There was to be no camaraderie on the pitch for the visitors from the West Midlands, however, as the Gunners eased past them 4-0.

A brace from Podolski and two late goals from Giroud and Cazorla saw them safely into round five. A 2-1 win over a Liverpool side in North London was revenge of sorts for the 5-1 trouncing they suffered at Anfield only eight days previously. Oxlade-Chamberlain and Podolski providing the goals to propel Wenger's side into a crucial sixth round tie at home against Roberto Martinez's Everton.

An early Ozil goal settled the nerves, and even as Lukaku levelled an Arteta penalty against his old side, two late Giroud goals booked a Wembley semi-final date against the holder Wigan Athletic.

A tense game was eventually won by Arsenal 4-2 on penalties after the 'Big F***ing German' grabbed a late equaliser to prevent the Gunners being another giant-killing scalp by an impressive Wigan side. The wild scenes of unrestrained joy as Cazorla's penalty went in belied the thought of a trophy at last arriving at Arsenal again.

And so to the final.

The author's All Guns Blazing Arsenal column in the *Islington Gazette* twenty-four hours before kick-off was prophetically headlined 'Arsenal FA Cup finals are never dull'.

Wenger, who reached his tenth final as Arsenal manager and his sixth FA Cup final, said with foresight before the game, 'Yes, I know we are favourites but what does being favourite mean in football? It doesn't guarantee you win the game.'

The opening eight minutes of this unforgettable game were living proof of his wise words.

Arsenal: Fabianski, Sagna, Koscielny, Mertesacker, Gibbs, Arteta, Cazorla, Ramsey, Ozil, Podolski, Giroud. Substitutes: Sanogo for Podolski, Wilshere for Cazorla, Rosicky for Ozil. Not used: Szczesny, Vermaelen, Monreal, Flamini.

Hull City: McGregor, Rosenior, Bruce, Chester, Meyler, Davies, Huddlestone, Fryatt, Livermore, Elmohamady, Quinn. Substitutes: McShane for Bruce, Aluko for Quinn, Boyd for Rosenior. Not used: Harper, Figueroa, Koren, Sagbo.

Referee: Lee Probert

Attendance: 89,345

On the morning of the game *The Sun* had printed:

There have been three Prime Ministers, Chelsea have had nine different managers, Wayne Rooney has grown hair, lost it and purchased a transplant, twitter has been created and gained over 500 million users in the 3,283 days since Arsenal last won the FA Cup.

Arsène Wenger, the team and every Arsenal fan worldwide was determined that run and the sneers would end.

Tigers' manager Steve Bruce, however, in Hull City's first-ever appearance in an FA Cup final, becoming the fifty-seventh different side to play in the final of the competition, proclaimed, 'If you're not an Arsenal fan, I'm sure the rest of the world will be rooting for Hull.'

Ex-Spurs midfielder Tom Huddleston had vowed to win the cup as much for Spurs fans as Hull fans. Tigers' David Myler scoffed, 'Arsenal can have their victory parade arranged already but we will be looking to beat them.'

Of which Paul Campbell, owner of cult Arsenal pie shop Piebury Corner had said to Sky Sports News the day before the game,

The planning of the victory parade was something Arsenal and the council had to do – it wasn't being overconfident or arrogant – I'm sure people at Hull had arranged the same – you can't have 200,000 people turn up without warning on Sunday morning if we win.

The morning itself was glorious. Clear blue skies that reminded all Gunners fans of the sunny days at Wembley when the 1971, 1979 and 1998 FA Cups were won.

Not that Hull City were going to let that fact stop them. On three minutes, the team from Humberside (minus their big-money strikers signed in the January transfer window, the Cup-tied Nikica Jelavic and Shane Long) were 1-0 up.

Bruce had started with what looked like a rather defensive minded starting eleven, with three centre-halves. However, the back line triumvirate played a large part in the astounding events of the opening eight minutes. From a Stephen Quinn corner, Huddlestone miscued the ball, which fell to James Chester. Chester, who was quoted at 66-1 as first goalscorer, showed quick feet in diverting the ball across Fabianski, playing what was to prove to be his last game for Arsenal.

Untrammelled joy ensued by the visitors from the North, matching the unrestrained celebrations on the pitch. More was to follow as Arsenal resembled a prize fighter who starts cold only to be brought to his knees before the fight has even started in earnest.

On eight minutes, Bruce's team were an improbable but deserved 2-0 up. As a free-kick was flighted into the Gunners' area with the defence looking disorganised and hesitant, Irishman Meyler's header was recovered by Quinn, who crossed it to the manger's son Alex. His underwhelming header evaded Fabianski but rebounded off the post into the path of another centre-back Curtis Davies.

Davies, who had written to twenty Premiership clubs as a youngster asking hopefully for a trial, receiving a written rejection from Arsenal (but being ignored by the majority of others), steered the ball home from an acute angle past the Gunners' despairing Polish custodian. As the ball crossed the line, Davis set off on a triumphant run, no doubt fuelled in a small part by the memory of that rejection.

Two-nil down with less than ten minutes on the clock would have floored many Wenger sides of the previous 3,283 days. Not so this vintage. Gibbs was alert in clearing off the goal line minutes later from the redoubtable Bruce junior. It was to prove a turning point as the Gunners gradually cast off their shock and began to display their technical superiority, even as Hull stalked their every move like the Tigers they were.

Yet Arsenal suddenly awoke from their slumbers, showing a fluidity that was absent in the early stages, as Santi Cazorla scored from one of the best free-kicks ever scored in a Wembley final on 17 minutes. Unfortunately, the drama that was to come rendered his superb effort forgotten in the maelstrom.

On the hour mark, Podolski had a valid claim for a penalty inexplicably turned down as Huddlestone bundled into him with extreme clumsiness. Shortly afterwards, Wenger switched the formation to a more direct 4-4-2, bringing on Yaya Sanogo for the German as the Gunners pressed for an equaliser.

To the relief of the Arsenal fans everywhere, City's resistance was finally broken by Koscielny on 72 minutes, who headed home from a Sagna corner.

Despite Gibbs, Giroud and Sanogo going close, the match went to extra time.

With both teams tiring, Wenger introduced Tomas Rosicky and Jack Wilshere for the final 15 minutes. To Arsenals delight, the bold move paid off as their fresh legs helped Arsenal clinch a late winner. On 109 minutes, a clever Giroud's backheel at the near post fed Ramsey to instinctively poke home past McGregor's near post.

Cue pandemonium from the Arsenal fans. Ramsey himself, in a neat nod to history, performed his version of a Charlie George 1971-style collapse.

As the minutes ticked by, ITV's co-commentator Andy Townsend was quick to castigate the silversmith, and by association Arsenal, when a shot of the craftsman carving details onto the Cup was aired in injury time tutting sanctimoniously, 'He's a bit premature.' Unfortunately, so was the ex-Chelsea player, as it was later revealed the accomplished expert was actually only engraving '2014' into the cup.

Despite a few heart-stopping moments towards the end, referee Probert eventually blew the whistle, signalling Wenger's team had won the 2014 FA Cup. After nine long years, Arsenal FC and Arsène Wenger had won silverware again.

A visibly delighted Wenger was candid in his relief, revealing his double substitution late in extra time was a deliberate gamble in a last-gasp attempt to win the game – thereby circumventing the lottery of a dreaded penalty shootout.

Speaking afterwards he said,

> I had a funny feeling not to go to penalties. I tried to go for it before the end. I tried desperately not to go to penalties because I did not have many players on the pitch who were specialists at it.
>
> It paid off but we had a horrible feeling for a long time in the game and in the end it was a relief. The job is how it finishes, all the rest nobody cares.
>
> Especially [taking off] Cazorla [was bold]. I must tell you Ozil I would not have put him on the penalty list, but Cazorla is a serious penalty taker and that's why I was hesitant.
>
> I was worried by the decision I was making because I had two strikers on the pitch. Jack is not a penalty taker, Rosicky is not a penalty taker. Giroud had cramp so it was difficult.

The man who was met with scepticism when he first arrived in England, the man who had revolutionised English football, the man who had brought style, panache, entertaining football and goals back to the club, the man who had who won two doubles, three League titles, and now five FA Cups, said plaintively with great emotion in his voice, 'This is the most important trophy of my career.'

Matchwinner Aaron Ramsey's goal was his sixteenth of the season. The twenty-three-year-old had rounded off his remarkable season with silverware. The modest Welshman, who had fought back from a near career-ending broken leg as well as criticism from high profile Arsenal fans, said afterwards,

> I'm just delighted to come back, make a big impact in a game and win the FA Cup. I had a few rash shots but I think I made up for it in the end. It was a great lay-off by Giroud.
>
> I shouted for it and he back-heeled it. The goalkeeper has a lot less time to react when you finish it first time. It was the most important goal of my time here.

Articulating the thoughts of all Gooners everywhere, hoping the first silverware in nine years would be a launch pad to a sustained League title challenge and a genuine Champions League run, he added, 'We can hopefully have an opportunity to win a few more things next season.'

The *Daily Telegraph* concluded in breathless admiration,

> Wenger was thrown in the air; soaked in champagne by his players afterwards and this kind of May sunshine had the feel of days gone-by also. So did the scoreline. So did the manner of all those goals. This was the finest FA Cup final for the new Wembley.

Arsenal chief executive Ivan Gazidis said,

> I thought it was a great day for Arsène. He's been through a lot and you can see that he lives this club – you can see how much he loves it and how much it means to him.
>
> To see him soaking wet and getting thrown up in the air – he was probably a bit nervous about that – but it was fantastic, it was really great!

One particular long-standing Arsenal season ticket holder, who had made the trip to Wembley, Guy Wiseman said,

> It was great to see the joy and relief on Arsène's face at the end. He celebrated like one of the players and deservedly so. One lad who sits in my row at the Emirates managed to get Arsène's tie, which was thrown into the crowd as we all sang 'there's only one Arsène Wenger'.

Guy from Hitchin, Hertfordshire, whose face repeatedly appeared on television, including the big screens inside the ground during the match – and who also featured prominently in montages detailing fans' celebrations on Arsenal iPlayer – added,

> Arsène took a lot of stick that season, including from Arsenal fans. But at that moment, whatever your view on Arsène Wenger, Gooners everywhere recognised that victory was for him as much as anyone.

The author had taken his seven-year-old son to the game. After the memorable finish and the equally memorable celebrations with the trophy, my wide-eyed Junior Gunner William said to me in wonder, 'Thanks for taking me dad – it was the best day ever.'

As a season ticket holder since the mid-1980s, after nine long years without a trophy, it certainly felt that way.

Acknowledgements

At the risk of sounding like an award-winning acceptance speech, there's a lot of people I have to thank for their help and support, not only for this book, but for me becoming a fully fledged journalist and author. John Francis, without whose encouragement, advice, wise counsel and belief when others faltered, I would not be a proud member of the fifth estate. Stephen Tudor of *The Daisy Cutter* and Dominic Bliss of *The Inside Left* for publishing me when no one else would. The genius that is James Brown and all the gang at *Sabotage Times*, not least Sam Diss and Tom Armstrong. Owen Blackhurst for his brutal honesty, even if he can't hold his drink. Two fine journalists in their different spheres, Owain Jones and Duncan Hamilton for their constant help. The deputy editor of the *Independent* and *Evening Standard,* Will Gore, for his backing, *Evening Standard* digital sports editor Amar Singh for his valuable advice on Fleet Street writing techniques, the legend that is Patrick Barclay for his unfailingly good humour and wonderfully articulated insights. Roz McKenzie and the Lambeth NCTJ, Joanne Butcher of the NUJ, and the JDF. Georgina Hill for her unflagging resourcefulness and patience. Sol Campbell for his time and help with the foreword, and for his passionate and articulate insights into Arsenal and Arsène Wenger, and in particular The Invincibles season, and for conveying the impression of a man who completely loves football. Ray Parlour for his humour and stories. Mike Francis and Kevin Whitcher of *The Gooner* for publishing my Arsenal ramblings in their fanzine, and for their initial backing with this project. All at Amberely Publishing – it goes without saying any errors, omissions or mistakes in this book are down to me. Thanks also to Dutch Arsenal fan Bart Boumans of the British Library, whose enthusiasm in helping me target my research knew no bounds. To all at the Highbury Barn, and all those friends, teammates, work colleagues, both old and new, and relatives who have supported me – the list is far too long to mention here but you know who you are – please accept my humble thanks and an offer of a pint next time we see each other. To Anne Aurousseau for her amazing bravery, which will always be an inspiration to me. To Jamie Street, Ben Street, Ellie Street and Olive Street. To my mother for her love, common sense and understanding, and my father, a tough but fair man, and one who is, and always will be my hero – not least for ensuring I was born to be an Arsenal fan – thanks for taking me to Highbury dad. And, of course, all my love to my three children who are already huge Gooners – Charlotte, William and Josie – whose inquisitive questions not least about the Gunners, and down-to-earth nature and wonderful words, sayings and conversations have made me such a proud and blessed parent. (And yes Josie, I fully agree – as boy bands go The Stone Roses are far better than One Direction.) Finally, to my partner Claire, without whose practical support this book would never have been written. I owe you so much, I only hope you can forgive me for my selfishness and absences during my long spells of writing, you truly have been my rock.